DEVELOPMENT

New Paradigms and Principles
for the Twenty-first Century

Edited by
Jo Marie Griesgraber and Bernhard G. Gunter

Pluto Press
LONDON • EAST HAVEN, CT
with
Center of Concern WASHINGTON, DC

First published 1996 by Pluto Press
345 Archway Road, London N6 5AA
and 140 Commerce Street,
East Haven, CT 06512, USA

British Library Cataloguing in Publication Data
A catalogue record for this book is available
from the British Library

ISBN 0 7453 1048 6 (hbk)

Library of Congress Cataloging in Publication Data
Development : new paradigms and principles for the twenty-first century
    / edited by Jo Marie Griesgraber and Bernhard G. Gunter
    p.   cm.   — (Rethinking Bretton Woods : v. 2)
    Includes bibliographical references and index.
    ISBN 0–7453–1048–6
    1. International Monetary Fund. 2. World Bank. 3. International
finance—History. 4. Economic development—History. 5. Twenty-
first century—Forecasts. I. Griesgraber, Jo Marie. II. Gunter,
Bernhard G., 1964–   . III. Series.
    HG3881.D435   1996
            338.9—dc20   95–38685
                                                                CIP

Designed, typeset and produced for Pluto Press by
Chase Production Services, Chipping Norton, OX7 5QR
Printed in the EC by T J Press, Padstow, England

Contents

Figures

Tables

This volume is dedicated to the memory of
Jorge Federico Sábato,
a co-sponsor of the Rethinking Bretton Woods project.
Jorge died on February 10, 1995 in a car accident in his
native Argentina. Jorge worked passionately for social
and economic justice in Argentina, and studied with great
energy and insight the implications for social justice
of economic globalization.

Preface

To explore a broad range of proposals for achieving more equitable, sustainable and participatory development, particularly
through the international financial institutions, the Center of Concern convened a conference in Washington, DC, from June 12–17,
1994. The conference was a part of the Rethinking Bretton Woods
project, which marked the 50th anniversary of the Bretton Woods,
New Hampshire, meeting that created the World Bank and the
International Monetary Fund (IMF) and laid the groundwork for
the General Agreement on Tariffs and Trade (GATT), succeeded
by the World Trade Organization (WTO) in 1995.

Conference participants came from 27 countries in Africa, Asia,
Australia, Europe and North and South America, and included
economists, historians, sociologists, lawyers, businesspeople,
political scientists, theologians and representatives of the Bretton
Woods institutions (BWIs). Their papers and discussions focused
on roles for the BWIs – the World Bank, the IMF and the soon-
to-be-established WTO – in initiating, assisting and sustaining
such development. This series of books originated as the prepara-
tory papers for that conference.

The project's 23 co-sponsors include people from academic and
non-governmental institutions in 18 countries; an advisory group
has members from nine countries. The lead organization, the
Center of Concern, is a Washington, DC-based social justice
research center founded in 1971 to analyze, educate and advocate
on issues of international development. Louis Goodman, Dean of
the School of International Service at The American University, a
project adviser and co-sponsor, hosted the conference.

This book is the result of the hard work and generosity of
many: the advisers and co-sponsors of 'Rethinking Bretton
Woods'; the funders, the John D. and Catherine T. MacArthur
Foundation, the Ford Foundation, the C.S. Mott Foundation, the
World Council of Churches, CEBEMO, Trocaire and CAFOD,
and their very competent staffs; the staff and interns of the
Center of Concern; the style editors Joan Leibman and Jane

Deren; the staff at Pluto Press, Roger van Zwanenberg *et al.*; but especially the intelligent and persistent John Walsh, who pulled it all together. The editors appreciate deeply the support and good humor of families: Shaw, Andrea, Stanley, David and Jesmin.

Jo Marie Griesgraber
Bernhard Gunter
Washington, DC
September 1995

List of Acronyms

AfDB	African Development Bank
ADB	Asian Development Bank
BWI	Bretton Woods institution
CFI	country futures indicator
EBRD	European Bank for Reconstruction and Development
G–7	Group of Seven
GATT	General Agreement on Tariffs and Trade
GEF	Global Environment Facility
GDP	Gross Domestic Product
GNP	Gross National Product
HDI	Human Development Index
IBRD	International Bank for Reconstruction and Development
IDB	Inter-American Development Bank
IFI	international financial institution
IMF	International Monetary Fund
ITO	International Trade Organization
LETS	local exchange trading system
MDB	multilateral development bank
MDP	Management Development Programme
NAFTA	North American Free Trade Agreement
NAIRU	non-accelerating inflation rate of unemployment
NGO	non-governmental organization
NORAD	Norwegian Agency for Development Cooperation
ODA	official development assistance
ODII	Organizing for Development, An International Institute
OECD	Organization for Economic Cooperation and Development
PPP	purchasing power parity
RDB	regional development bank
SAL	structural adjustment loan
SAP	structural adjustment program
SEC	Securities and Exchange Commission
SECAL	sectoral adjustment loan
SNA	System of National Accounts
TNC	transnational corporation
UNCSD	United Nations Commission on Sustainable Development
UNDP	United Nations Development Programme

UNEP   United Nations Environment Programme
UNICEF United Nations International Children's Emergency Fund
UNSIA   United Nations Security Insurance Agency
WTO   World Trade Organization

Introduction

The Cold War's denouement brought to an end an era that
stretched nearly 50 years. Toward the end of World War II, international institutions were established in an effort to avoid repeat-
ing the horrors of the Great Depression and the mistakes of the
punitive Versailles Treaty that concluded World War I. There was
a magnanimity to these solutions. In the economic realm, free
trade, stable currency regimes and the rebuilding of allies and
enemies alike would prevent a second Great Depression. At the
Conference at Bretton Woods, New Hampshire, in 1944, the
Allies set up the International Monetary Fund (IMF) to ensure a
stable international currency regime that would facilitate international trade; the still-born International Trade Organization was
to have further encouraged free trade while promoting social and
labor standards. The World Bank would recycle money from
wealthy countries, first to war-torn Europe and Japan, and then to
the poorer nations. While the Marshall Plan provided the lion's
share of funding for post-war reconstruction, the World Bank soon
commenced its work of funding infrastructure projects in developing countries, beginning in Chile in 1948. On the political front,
the United Nations incorporated virtually all the world's then-
sovereign states under a single peak international organization.

But the semblance of global unity soon developed a major fis-
sure as the world divided into two blocs during the Cold War.
East and West, led respectively by the former Soviet Union and
the United States, proceeded to divide the rest of the world
between them. There were satellite states and spheres of influence
and 'cold battles' where surrogate states fought, lest the giant
states resort to nuclear war. As Roy Culpeper explains in Chapter
3, the World Bank and the IMF – the Bretton Woods institutions
(BWIs) – became instruments of the West, while the United
Nations was rendered ineffective because of the balance of political forces between the two blocs.

Only with the collapse of the Berlin Wall, symbol of the mono-
lithic Communist Eastern bloc, could fresh questions arise and

xiii

new values reach greater global attention. In this volume, we turn our attention to the emergence of a new set of values clustering around the concept of development.

Whereas Volume 1 in this series, 'Promoting Development: Effective Global Institutions for the Twenty-first Century', was full of pragmatic recommendations for reforming the BWIs, this volume steps back to recognize and to articulate the profound shift in ways of thinking about development. This shift might be called a 'revolution', meaning a full turning about, or 'radical', as in pulling out by, or changing, the roots. In psychological terms it might be a 'gestalt switch'; in religious terms it would be a 'conversion'. We prefer to call it a 'paradigm shift'. In the scientific community, the paradigm is an organizing framework that is shaped by the accepted truths of the discipline and which identifies the remaining puzzles to be explored to round out that framework. As Sixto Roxas explains in the opening chapter, and Turid Sato and William Smith reiterate in Chapter 5, for Thomas Kuhn, an 'intellectual paradigm' refers to the 'analytical method that forms the basis of a "school" of scientists for whom the application of the method is 'normal science.'[1]

The volume title adds the notion of 'Principles' to 'Paradigm' because the paradigm shift includes a movement from covert or implicit norms to overt or explicit norms. The earlier view of development was restricted to economic growth, usually measured by Gross National Product (GNP) per capita. It alleged to be value-free, based on economic tenets. The new approach to development includes the values of equity, participation and environmental sustainability, as well as improving physical well-being.

A definition of development according to the new paradigm emerged at the June 1994 conference on Rethinking Bretton Woods. As described in *Rethinking Bretton Woods: Conference Report and Recommendations*, development is considered to be 'a multi-dimensional, people-centered process':

> The goal of development is to create conditions that will enable each human being to realize her/his potential for political, social, and economic fulfillment in a manner consistent with the common good. Individual rights, duties, and participation are central to this process and to its goal. The first priority is the eradication of poverty, empowering people to gain a measure of

---

1 Sixto Roxas, chapter 1: 'Principles for Institutional Reform', note 1, p. 22.

control over their own lives and to obtain the resources to meet their basic needs in an ecologically sustainable manner. Genuine development is essentially a grassroots, bottom-up process, growing from the base with local communities being key players. Economic activity should be managed by human beings, within the bounds of the fragile and exhaustible environment. The market may be a means to achieving these goals, but it is not an end in itself.

Decision-making procedures in the development process must embody the principles of participation, transparency, accountability, and subsidiarity.[2]

As the essays in this volume elaborate, development is about the total person living both in a community and in a limited ecosystem. Participation is a core aspect of development. That participation takes place through diverse human organizations, including but not limited to the nation state, transnational organizations and subnational organizations, which may themselves act across national borders. This volume, like *Rethinking Bretton Woods: Conference Report and Recommendations*, endorses the principle of subsidiarity to explain the preferred mode of interaction among these diverse organizations. According to subsidiarity, decisions should be made at the lowest possible level, even while acknowledging that some problems are community-wide in scope, others nation-wide, and still others global.

Throughout the volume, the various authors demonstrate many common values as captured in the new paradigm language; however, they offer diverse intellectual and pragmatic steps for moving toward the common goal.

In the opening essay, 'Principles for Institutional Reform', Sixto Roxas, director of the Foundation for Community Organization and Management Technology in the Philippines, explains important aspects of the process that resulted in the old development paradigm, and proposes principles and concrete steps to achieve the evolving new paradigm. Roxas, like Hazel Henderson in Chapter 6, 'Changing Paradigms and Indicators: Implementing Equitable, Sustainable and Participatory Development', highlights the critical role of economic indicators. Measures of national wealth such as the Gross National Product (GNP) grew out of wartime

---

2 Jo Marie Griesgraber (ed.), *Rethinking Bretton Woods: Conference Report and Recommendations* (Washington, DC: Center of Concern, 1994), p. 1.

efforts to measure productivity. As Henderson observes, 'we measure what we treasure'. And if something was not – or could not easily be – measured, it was assumed that it had *no value*. This may have been tolerable during the World War II emergency years, and it endured through the Cold War. However, it is no longer tenable to assign *no value* to clean air, old-growth forests, biodiversity, women's work, or beauty.

The United Nations, the World Bank and the IMF became institutions for promulgating the uniform national accounting system, and the values that lay behind it. The World Bank went beyond that to become a centralized training center for government bureaucrats, who learned not only what to measure, but the corollary values and *modus operandi* of the World Bank. As Roxas, a retired merchant bank and government official, observed at close range, government bureaucrats, employees of the Bank and the IMF, and private bankers came to share not only the same accounting system, but also the same schools and friends; even their jobs became interchangeable.

Roxas explains how the basis of the old accounting system was the firm; his radical alternative accounting system would use the community as the core unit of accounting. For Roxas, community implies a limited and specific ecosystem.

International law professors Daniel Bradlow and Claudio Grossman of the Washington College of Law at The American University bring their considerable practical and theoretical expertise on the legal aspects of international debt and human rights law to Chapter 2, 'Adjusting the Bretton Woods Institutions to Contemporary Realities'. They contrast the mandates of the Bretton Woods institutions with current reality. These institutions were established as inter-governmental agencies, to work on discrete problems. But today, it is neither possible nor appropriate to ignore non-state actors, from transnational corporations through non-governmental organizations, and problems have become increasingly complex and interconnected. While staying largely within the parameters of the BWIs' Articles of Agreement, Bradlow and Grossman propose: greater coordination between the BWIs and specialized UN agencies; requiring the BWIs to operate consistent with universal legal principles such as those found in the Universal Declaration of Human Rights and various environmental treaties, as well as in specific protocols signed by borrower governments; and increasing the role, accountability, and transparency of nation states themselves.

In Chapter 3, 'Multilateral Development Banks: Towards a New Division of Labor', Roy Culpeper, vice-president and director of research on international debt and finance of Canada's prestigious North–South Institute, suggests implications of the new development paradigm for the multilateral development banks (MDBs) – here, the World Bank plus three regional development banks (RDBs), the Inter-American Development Bank (IDB), the African Development Bank (AfDB), and the Asian Development Bank (ADB). The principles of participation and subsidiarity should lead to greater devolution of responsibility from the centralized World Bank to the RDBs and the national governments themselves. Greater decentralization, along with more accountability and transparency, should enable the MDBs and the governments to encourage diversity of approaches to development problem-solving.

BothENDs' Lisa Jordan, former Director of GLOBE-US (Global Legislators Organization for a Balanced Environment) and legislative aide in the US Congress, locates the various authors among the progressive movement. In her essay, 'The Bretton Woods Challengers', she identifies the 'alternative normative' camp and the 'structuralist' or 'global Keynesian' camp as two ends of a spectrum of progressive thought. While there are no pure types, Roxas portrays well the former, and Bradlow and Grossman the latter. The principle of subsidiarity shows the potential to bridge the distance between the two. The chapter begins to offer solutions to the problems of participation and representation contained in the proposals of the 'global Keynesians' and to the seeming obliviousness to the reality of an already-global economy that characterizes the reform proposals of the 'alternative normative' camp.

In 'The New Development Paradigm: Organizing for Implementation', Turid Sato and William Smith, co-directors of Organizing for Development, An International Institute (ODII), present the findings from a global workshop held in September 1993 that explored ways to implement the new development paradigm, which stresses comprehensive participation and partnership. This chapter offers a recapitulation of Kuhn's 'paradigm shift', and presents an 'exemplar' of the new paradigm in practice: Thailand's Five Star Partnership Program integrated and coordinated the efforts of government, NGOs, private sector, religious communities and academic organizations, thereby forming a support circle to help facilitate community/provincial development. Development agencies and governments – the bureaucracies through which official resources are channelled – are called on to become less controlling and give room for civic society to participate as partners. The support of the Norwegian, Japanese and Dutch governments for the workshop upon which this chapter is based indicates incipient support for the new paradigm from the official sector, as well as civil society.

In the concluding chapter, 'Changing Paradigms and Indicators: Implementing Equitable, Sustainable and Participatory Development', futurist Hazel Henderson, with her usual inimitable virtuosity, elaborates on the twin themes of paradigms and indicators, describing the possibilities and practice from the community through the global level. On the latter, she proposes a mechanism for providing independent financing for a more independent and effective United Nations via the Tobin tax on speculative financial transactions, a mechanism that at the same time would offer the benefit of slowing the speculative 'global casino'. Henderson's chapter appropriately combines her visionary and pragmatic sides, apparent throughout her career. She has held the Horace Albright Chair at the University of California at Berkeley, and served on the original Presidential Advisory Council of the US Office of Technology Assessment. Currently, Henderson serves on the Business Council for the UN World Summit on Social Development (BUSCO, Paris), the Task Force on Efficient Capital Markets of the Business Council for Sustainable Development (Geneva), and as a Commissioner of the Global Commission to Fund the UN (Washington, DC).

As Jordan so astutely observes, there is great diversity in the approaches among those who endorse putting a new development paradigm into practice. This diversity is itself a strength and a richness. A paradigm that would embrace the whole person in community, circumscribed by the finite ecosystem of the planet, must also embrace diversity of styles. Indeed, a fundamental flaw of the old paradigm is its rigidity, that would cram all peoples and cultures into a single solution, with one definitive set of numbers.

1. Principles for Institutional Reform

Sixto K. Roxas

INTRODUCTION

The conferences at Bretton Woods in 1944 and San Francisco in 1945 institutionalized more than just a fund, a bank and a complex of international agencies. They embodied an intellectual paradigm which became a universal worldview and an ideology. The paradigm was the synthesis of neoclassical and Keynesian economics, the so-called neoclassical synthesis. The ideology was capitalism.[1]

Serving the interests of governments, major corporations, and financial institutions of Western industrial countries, this paradigm and ideology became the blueprint for a process of globalization that can be described in four stages:

1. post-war restoration,

2. synthesis of neoclassical and Keynesian economics,

3. political de-colonization and economic re-colonization,

4. globalization of the enterprise system.

This chapter analyzes these four stages, evaluates the world scene after 50 years of globalization, and describes the kind of institutional principles necessary for equitable, sustainable and participatory development.

1

THE GLOBALIZATION PROCESS

The Post-War Restoration

The United States emerged from World War II as the only major industrial country with its productive capacity intact. It proceeded first to assist its allies, but soon extended its assistance to former enemies as well through the Marshall Plan. The offers of aid were accepted only by countries in western Europe, who established the Organization for European Economic Cooperation in 1948 to implement the European Recovery Programme, in cooperation with the American Economic Cooperation Administration. All countries of the soon-established Soviet bloc were excluded. Thus, the post-war restoration entailed a political and economic bipolarization of the world. The Bretton Woods institutions (BWIs) embodied the economic principles of the neoclassical synthesis (see next section), which was not acceptable to the Soviet Union. However, the Soviets did subscribe to the UN Charter, even though the United Nations embodied the political principles of liberal democracy. Besides this bipolarization of the world (which ended on November 9, 1989, when the Berlin Wall came down), the BWIs embodied also the restoration of the nineteenth-century economic order.

Synthesis of Neoclassical and Keynesian Economics

In his famous 1944 analysis, *The Great Transformation*, Karl Polanyi described nineteenth-century Europe as resting on four institutions that 'determined the characteristic outlines of the history of our civilization':[2]

1. a balance-of-power system,
2. an international gold standard,
3. a self-regulating market, and
4. a liberal state.

Of the four, the self-regulating market was the central mechanism, 'the fount and matrix of the system', giving Europe the specific character of its civilization. The gold standard gave the system its international scope. The balance-of-power system was a super-structure erected upon the gold standard that relied in part on the gold standard for its own viability; the liberal state was itself a creature of the self-regulating market.

2

The key to the system was the belief that the laws governing the market economy were of the same category as the laws Newton had discovered determined the motions of the universe. They were natural laws that could be relied on to ensure that atomistic individual behavior of human beings, all pursuing their own happiness, would in the end harmonize with the imperatives of universal order.

The best policy for nations and states was to leave these laws to operate by themselves, without interference. Indeed, the primary obligation of states was to ensure that nothing interfered with the free and unhampered workings of the market. And for a hundred years, it seemed, the system produced prodigious results – the 'European Miracle'.[3] After the Napoleonic Wars, Europe enjoyed a hundred years of relative peace, during which no Great Power wars seriously disrupted economic and social life.[4] In that atmosphere of relative tranquility, European countries followed Great Britain in industrializing their economies.[5] (The respite from intra-European Great Power wars did not mean an end to European involvement in armed conflict. During this period, European and North American wars of conquest against less developed nations intensified.)[6]

In 1944, as the architects of Bretton Woods deliberated on the strategy for reconstruction after World War II, historical upheavals and theoretical 'revolutions' had already established a change in worldview. Four dramatic events contributed to this change: World War I (1914–18) had brought the hundred years' peace to an explosive end. The 1917 revolution in Russia had established a Communist regime. The world entered into the worst depression in history in 1929. The attempt to re-establish the gold standard ended in frustration and in its total demise in 1931.

In the intellectual arena, the belief in a self-regulating market mechanism waned. The ideas and crude instruments for national planning were already in the air before the outbreak of World War I. Put on a war footing after 1914, nations were forced into national planning, and the forms remained after the war. Disenchantment with the automatic market followed the depression and there was an increased clamor for state planning interventions. In 1926, Keynes wrote his essay entitled 'The End of Laissez-Faire'. Ten years later, his 'General Theory' launched the 'Keynesian Revolution' that became the theoretical basis of the 'Mixed Economy'.[7] Private enterprises should continue to be the prime movers of an economy and markets should be left to operate freely, but governments had a role to ensure the adequacy and wide distribution of purchasing power, thereby maintaining a sufficient level of effective demand to keep economies operating at full employment.

3

The chaotic state of the global economic system in the period between the two world wars left a deep impression on economists and economic policymakers: the competitive devaluations, raising of tariff and non-tariff controls on international trade, 'beggar-thy-neighbor' policies, and attempts to solve domestic crises by classical remedies of budget cuts and monetary constraints caused widespread deflation and, eventually, world-wide depression.

The Bretton Woods covenant implemented the neoclassical synthesis, committing the institutions to a particular blueprint of world development and transformation. The essential propositions of this blueprint were:

- atomistic individualism: the individual as the all-important unit of society;

- hedonism and utilitarianism: the individual's right to seek maximum personal happiness;

- social good as the arithmetic sum of individual satisfactions, that is, the greatest good of the greatest number;

- society as the result of a contract among individuals;

- private property, founded on individualism;

- the rights to life, liberty and property, essential to the individual, as the basis of the democratic polity. The state, like society, is the creature of a contract that individuals enter into to create an environment in which those rights can be protected and exercised with security. The state's primary responsibility is to protect those rights; and

- the economic system as the organization within which those rights translate into free exchanges that maximize the gains of individuals from their use of their resources. The market is the forum through which individuals achieve exchanges that maximize their satisfactions. Therefore, the market is the democratic institution *par excellence*, since it is the primary means through which society achieves the greatest good of the greatest number.

Walter Russell Mead aptly characterizes the strategy embodied in the Bretton Woods system as 'low-octane' Keynesianism, 'an economic expansion in which growth of purchasing power was not to

4

exceed the increase in production. The Keynesian stress on demand and expansion was present, but so too were institutional barriers against unbalanced growth and the resulting inflation.'8

Hence the four primary goals established for the Bretton Woods system were full employment, price stability, economic growth and balance-of-payments equilibrium. The system design assumed that each member country would have a modern, capitalistic, market economy with a developed private business sector, reasonably free product and factor markets, a commercial banking system, a central bank and a finance ministry that managed the fiscal budget. An economic planning ministry and a reasonably developed financial market were also desirable. The corporation laws, accounting and audit ground rules, and the system of macroeconomic accounts would have to able to handle at least the following: money and banking statistics and money-supply accounting; foreign trade and invisibles accounting to complete a balance-of-payments recording system; national income and product accounts and series on prices, physical production, income and employment, gross sales and investments.

In the developing countries, these assumed institutions were generally limited to the colonial import–export enclaves – the capital cities and the mining, logging and plantation towns. These represented enclaves in the sense that they were more closely linked to the metropolitan countries than to their own hinterland.

In such enclaves the economy operated according to the macro-model. Households in the cash economy sold their services to enterprise and government and received their incomes, which they spent on consumer goods and consumer durables. They saved a portion with banks or invested in securities. Enterprises sold consumer and capital goods to households, other enterprises and governments. They paid wages and salaries to labor, staff and managers, paid dividends, borrowed from banks or raised funds from the securities markets, and invested in inventory and new plant. Their export and import transactions were recorded at customs and the records were tabulated in aggregate trade statistics. Invisible flows were intermediated through the banks and were recorded in the corresponding capital accounts. Enterprise, government, institutional and household accounts were consolidated into national income and product accounts and were published as the series on national incomes and product. Banks took funds in the form of checking, savings and time-deposit accounts, maintained reserves prescribed by the central bank and gave loans and invested in government securities – transactions that might take place in New York or London.

Where such institutions were absent, the Bretton Woods instruments were of little use. In pre-capitalistic and non-monetized societies, obviously, purchasing power is not created by the simple infusion of money and credit. It avails little to prime pumps in societies where there are no modern economic pumps, or to fuel engines of demand where capitalistic engines have to be designed, fabricated and installed.

It was to be expected, therefore, that after a decade and a half of seeking the real-world niche where they could perform in accord with the expectations of their designers and constituents, the BWIs settled on the task of creating a world that supported their worldview and was susceptible to their methods and tools of operation.

Political De-colonization and Economic Re-colonization

At the time of the Bretton Woods conference, the 'First World' comprised the countries that had achieved industrialization by the time of World War I – the so-called metropolitan countries. Most of what came to be known as the 'Third World' of underdeveloped countries were still colonies of those countries, except for Latin America. But even in the case of most of Latin America, which had been independent since the turn of the nineteenth century, the economic hegemony of the industrialized countries held sway.

In the European and American colonies in the Middle East, Africa and Asia, independence movements were in full momentum. Still, the industrialized metropolitan countries dominated the economies of these countries, which produced primary commodities. In the discussions of post-war plans, it was generally assumed that the fate of the non-industrialized countries and colonies would be subsumed under the interests of the western metropolitan countries. Indeed, initially the BWIs were not particularly concerned with their development.[9]

While non-industrialized regions had been victims of war devastation, and therefore shared in the problems of monetary disorganization and reconstruction, their underdeveloped state meant that mere restoration of pre-war structure would address only a small portion of their deeper problems. Still, in the discussion of the charter of the International Bank for Reconstruction and Development (IBRD), representatives from less developed countries had some success in inserting development among the purposes of the bank. This would become the BWIs' focus only after reconstruction in the metropolitan states was completed.

Moreover, although a political de-colonialization occurred in the decades following World War II, the neoclassical synthesis as described above implied economic re-colonialization, especially if seen in connection with the policies of the multinational corporations.

Globalization of the Enterprise System

The system that became preponderant was quite different from the classic vision of a world of small producers and traders bidding with one another to offer the best products and services to millions of sovereign consumers in a free competitive market.

It is important to understand that in classical economics, at least up to the time of David Ricardo, the unit players were individual persons. For Richard Cantillon (whose work antedated Adam Smith by nearly half a century) the entrepreneur, a natural person, played the pivotal role in economics, that is, the enterpriser and not the enterprise.[10] This was also the case in the analysis of Adam Smith. The analytical models reflected the realities of history; large-scale enterprise did not become preponderant until the late nineteenth and early twentieth centuries.

In 1932, Adolf A. Berle, Jr and Gardiner C. Means drew attention to this fundamental change in the industrialized economies:

> The corporation has, in fact, become both a method of property tenure and a means of organizing economic life. Grown to tremendous proportions, there may be said to have evolved a 'corporate system' – as there was once a feudal system – which has attracted to itself a combination of attributes and powers, and has attained a degree of prominence entitling it to be dealt with as a major social institution.[11]

The critical consequence of this development was the separation of management from ownership.

With this separation, capitalism assumed a different character from that described in classical economics, in which decisions were made by individual managing proprietors. With the emergence of the large corporate enterprise, a fundamental change took place. In the words of Alfred Chandler, Jr 'the world received a new kind of capitalism – one in which the decisions about current operations, employment, output, and the allocation of resources for future operations were made by salaried managers who were not owners of the enterprise.' They were 'a new subspecies of economic man' who

7

was then to provide the 'central dynamic for continuing economic growth and transformation'.[12]

In 1967, John Kenneth Galbraith had already described this emergent mega-corporate, calling it the 'Industrial System', and naming the new managerial class it spawned, 'the Technostructure'. To the new world order it created, he gave the threatening label of the 'New Industrial State'. The awesome power of this system is glossed over by propaganda that still paints an idyllic picture of free-market capitalism in terms of millions of small traders competing with one another to offer the best service to the sovereign consumers in a freely competitive market.[13]

The large enterprises that emerged from the later industrial revolution continue as our contemporary industrial giants, the transnational corporations. This was one of the conclusions of Alfred D. Chandler, Jr in studying the 200 largest industrial enterprises of the United States, Great Britain and Germany.[14]

On the threshold of the next century and the next millennium, the world has been molded largely by the designs of this industrial system. The ruling paradigm has not been the market, but rather, for-profit enterprise economics. Markets operated long before the first industrial revolution.[15] The predominance of the sector-specialized, profit-guided enterprise as the central actor and decision maker defines this awesome force.

In a process of pre-emption well-described by Galbraith, this enterprise system has put in its service both national governments and the international agencies that the national governments formed. The Bretton Woods institutions became some of its most effective advocates. Development became identified with the entry of these enterprises into any territory and the establishment of their branches, from which they could source cheaper materials, labor and energy, or enjoy substantial tax and other benefits.

In Third World countries this generally had a dual effect. In the first place, it provided opportunities for employment of professionals, managerial and supervisory personnel and work demanding various skills for young men and women. But in the second place, it also resulted in displacement and dislocation of farmers, fishers and communities whose lands were appropriated – to build not only the plants of these enterprises, but also the infrastructure to serve their production needs, as well as the commercial offices, residential apartments, golf courses and recreation facilities that were part of the lifestyle that they introduced. More important, by the demonstration effect of the lifestyle, the more traditional populations were enticed to adopt a level of living that could not be democratized in the local economy.

The enterprises were desired for the first effect. As a result, governments and communities vied for their favors. The second effect was deemed only the result of not enough of these investments taking place. It was believed that the solution would be to campaign more vigorously for the establishment of more of these enclaves. The effects they had on lifestyle were deemed part of the process of bringing the local communities into the twentieth century.

A force that has wrought the spectacular transformations of the last half-century cannot simply be rejected. But we must understand precisely where the theory has gone wrong. How has it spawned unbelievable growth and elevation of lifestyles on the one hand, and massive marginalization and widespread 'immiseration' on the other?

Seen from the point of view of organization, such results would be expected from a system whose dynamic force springs from individual persons and organizations selecting from the range of needs in every society only those that yield the most attractive gains. It is analogous to the way an opportunist miner picks from an ore body only those with the highest assay. The effect is to leave beyond economic recovery the 'low-grade' ore. In societies, the result is to leave beyond feasible servicing the vital needs of most of the population – health, education, environmental preservation, care for the poor and the disabled. The result is evident precisely in the polarization of humanity into a minority enjoying unprecedented opulence and a large majority facing increasingly unmanageable problems.

As enterprise became larger and more powerful, it succeeded more effectively in creaming the best resources for its narrow purposes. The residual chores of society for the growing numbers of marginalized people fell on governments first. As a result, governments have had to grow bigger and bigger, becoming at the same time less efficient and less able to cope. Private enterprise then began to form non-profit foundations to remedy at the margin the pathological effects produced by the enterprise economy's mainstream operations. In more recent decades, civil society itself has found the need to organize and cope with the dislocations and misery that 'progress' has left in its wake.

THE GLOBAL SCENE AFTER 50 YEARS OF GLOBALIZATION

It is not necessary to elaborate on all the ways in which the BWIs joined forces with the governments, large corporations and financial institutions of the developed countries to establish the hegemony of the ruling economic order.[16] Theory became ideology and ideology became a blueprint for transforming the still 'undeveloped' world.[17] We need only to point to certain key elements of the campaign.

The establishment of a complex of international agencies and institutions – including the United Nations and its regional commissions, and the BWIs themselves – created opportunities for professionals (economists, engineers, lawyers, accountants and finance people) to enter the ranks of the new international civil service. In the meantime, the newly independent developing countries were establishing the apparatus of the Western enterprise economy – including central banks, government budget departments and finance or treasury ministries, central planning offices and statistics departments. In staffing these, there was a premium on professionals trained in Western universities and carrying degrees in economics and Western-style statistics.

Prepared by technical personnel from the United Nations and the BWIs, the design of the new national monetary, financial and economic statistics therefore conformed to the model. Country statistical offices were organized to fill the pro-forma tables of these agencies. An accounting system carries with it a whole philosophy and theory; once an accounting system is adopted by an organization, it builds into the logic of its operation – by accepting the system as the mode for assessing its performance – the theory implicit in the system.

Thus, one indicator of the scope of acceptance of the theory underlying the system of national accounts is its adoption by national governments as the official basis for measuring their economic performance. Tracking the history of national income and product accounting in effect tracks the success of the proselytizing work.[18]

The BWIs combined with the international banking community, the world of *haute finance*, to wield tremendous influence in the global propagation of the ruling ideology. This whole network of modern enterprise enclaves forms an interlinked world system, which is really a civilization. It has powerful methods of acculturation and recruitment to build up a growing corps of people whose education and development is determined by the opportunities offered by the enclaves.

Professionals such as finance people, engineers, architects, accountants and medical practitioners cater to the modern enclaves, where alone their skills apply. Primary production provides the export earnings that pay for imports to sustain the enclaves in their Western lifestyle. Local industries are subsidiaries, joint ventures or licensees of transnationals like Proctor & Gamble and Unilever, or franchised by McDonalds, Shakeys or 7-Eleven. These enclaves, then, represent the staging areas for the development model. Development is equated with projects to expand the production of these enclaves, replicate them in other areas and diversify their output, and with policies that render the developing countries more attractive and more accessible to foreign investors. The household population is acculturated by formal education and the media to adopting the lifestyle. The enclaves are also the seats of political power. Governments and the political leaders must relate to the constituencies in these centers – the economic and intellectual leaders, the property owners, the religious hierarchy, the owners and editorial staff of the media.

It has become typical over the last three decades that each new government in a developing country launches a program of exchange liberalization, removal of import and investment restrictions, an austerity budget, and an economic growth program relying on an aggressive export drive and packages of incentives for the entry of direct and portfolio investments. This happens even when a new leadership has won election on a platform severely criticizing the policies and programs of an administration essentially following the same line.

This consistency is an index of how successfully the BWIs have staffed the career ranks of the civil service in these countries with technocrats who are thoroughly steeped in the paradigm and firm believers in its tenets. Regardless of the platform that won the election, the leaders of a new government need to have a highly sophisticated grasp of alternative strategies if they are to launch a program that departs radically from the advice of the senior technocrats, which is invariably: follow the prescriptions of the IMF and World Bank.

The BWIs have succeeded in building up a potent network of advocates among technocrats, political-level ministers and their deputies in the central banks and the planning ministries, budget offices and treasuries. Recruitment to the regular staff of the BWIs or serving as consultants to them are very attractive prospects. One of the sources of the growing influence of these institutions is the fact that as governments change, nationals working with the BWIs become likely candidates for recruitment back into the governments in their countries. The possibility of moving back to the BWIs if things do not work out politically at home or if there is another change of government, is a comfortable safety net. In this manner, over the years the BWIs have built up a powerful world-wide constituency. For their annual meetings, the BWIs have made a point of inviting retired ministers and the key private bankers of the member countries, promoting a feeling of camaraderie.

The global scene after 50 years of this process is best described by quoting the UN Development Program's (UNDP) *Human Development Report 1994*:

> What emerges is an arresting picture of unprecedented human progress and unspeakable human misery, of humanity's advance on several fronts mixed with humanity's retreat on several others, of a breathtaking globalization of prosperity side by side with a depressing globalization of poverty. As is so common in human affairs, nothing is simple and nothing is settled for ever.[19]

Business has emerged as the most powerful organization in the world. Its methods have come to stand for everything that is hard-nosed and rigorously efficient. Its methods have become the exemplar for all institutions, and 'business-like' has become equated with systematic, orderly and disciplined behavior. Its language has become currency in all of human activity which must have clear products, cater to markets, be cost-efficient and show returns at the 'bottom line'.

But the human condition is shrouded in deep shadows. Of 5.5 billion people on earth, 1.1 billion are over-consumers who use 80 per cent of the world's carrying capacity; 1.1 billion are poor peasants, fishing artisans, ethnic minorities, women and children who live below the poverty line; and 3.3 billion live at subsistence and barely over-subsistence levels. The richest billion people command 60 times the income of the poorest billion.

The planet is already manifesting clear signs of serious ecological damage at local and global levels. The planet's situation and the condition of humanity on it dictate the imperatives for the next century and the new millennium. We must be clear, first of all, precisely what they are: if we are faced with a full earth, then humanity as a whole must pursue a sustainable lifestyle and use technology in a way that preserves the planet's capacity.

We must understand how the imperatives are translated into a suitable global organization. What does this mean? The distribution of responsibilities among unit organizations, and the exercise of those responsibilities by the micro-decision units, must have built into them criteria that ensure, when all the micro-decisions are added up, that the resulting total stays within the planet's sustainable limits. Sustainability means drawing from the planet only the material and energy resources which preserve the integrity of its life-support capability for perpetual use of all future generations, while securing for each current generation an equitable and just distribution of the perquisites of a full, happy and peaceful life and the opportunities for improvement and development.

A world system in which the major resource-allocating decisions are directly made or powerfully influenced by today's successful for-profit enterprises obviously will not correspond to the organizational configuration that responds to global sustainable development imperatives. Of the many points that may be argued for this claim, one is especially telling. Each organization unit should speak for and protect an allotted portion of the planet's ecosystem. By definition, enterprise has no allegiance to territory. Its ultimate development is precisely defined as transnationality, which means the shedding of responsibility for any specific portion of the planet, a transcending of responsibility for the earth. Nothing in the enterprise's resource-allocating logic covers a concern for staying within the limits of the planet's carrying capacity. The lifestyle introduced is precisely one that cannot be democratized globally without bringing on the global disaster that the sustainability strategy is attempting to avert.

The imperatives of national and planetary sustainability, even survival, require business to place the concerns of communities and the NGOs in the mainstream. In turn, communities and NGOs need to develop the organization, technology and managerial skills that have made business so powerful. For business to find a sustainable course, it must fit its operations to the dictates of ecological integrity and social equity. For communities and NGOs, the fight for environment and justice must be reconciled with material productivity and organizational efficiency. Both views must converge in a genuine partnership if the planet is to survive.

NECESSARY NEW INSTITUTIONAL PRINCIPLES

The imperatives have to be made practical and operational. How is this to be accomplished? The elements that have made business the overriding historical force in the past 50 years provide a pattern to follow – communities must be empowered by imitation.

13

What is needed to offset the enterprise paradigm is a 'communitarian paradigm' founded on a different set of postulates:

- The *ruling order* is founded on the philosophy of individualism – the idea that the person is fulfilled as an individual, maximizing satisfaction through the use of all the resources of the earth.

  The *new order* must be based on the idea that the individual is fulfilled in harmony with the whole of creation – in community with one's own and other living species and in a manner that uses inanimate nature sustainably.

- The *ruling science* is reductionist, assuming that nature can be understood totally by the analysis of its parts and tends to revert to equilibrium states, that its behavior can be extrapolated by linear approximations, and that its dynamic motion traces reversible paths. Further, these laws are considered equally applicable to the behavior of human beings and their institutions.

  The *new science* must be holistic and systemic – based on the principle that the whole is greater than its parts, that non-equilibrium states are the rule rather than the exception, that paths of evolution are irreversible over time, that the emergence of life and human consciousness means organic processes and human management predominate over mechanistic forces in the continuing process of evolution, and ultimately that this is a moral and not a mechanical universe.

- The *ruling technology* maximizes dependence on fabricated artifacts based on massive energy inputs from fossil fuels, generating a wide variety of products designed to satisfy ever more specialized wants that are increasingly differentiated by conditioning from an incessant barrage of clever communications transmitted through hardware of ever greater sophistication.[20]

  The *new technology* must emerge out of the combined revision of consumer lifestyles that consciously evaluate the appropriateness of need-satisfiers according to the nature of fundamental human needs to achieve more sustainable consumption baskets and engineering designs that mimic nature's production modes.

- In the *ruling economic and social organization*, the profit-enterprise is the paradigm of organization units, its profit-seeking logic is the law of behavior, and the mechanism of free, competitive markets is the pre-eminent basis for the valuations that determine optimizing choices.

In the *new sustainable world*, the ecosystem, meaning the community of living populations in their natural habitats, must be the ruling economic and social organization and its life-supporting net output, the measure of welfare. The criteria and mechanisms for priority-setting valuations and for the setting of prices that determine mutuality of benefits must reflect these valuations rather than exclusively the valuations of profit-maximizing sector-specialized enterprises.

• The *enterprise logic* is rendered operational in the accounting system that has developed and become universally standard for measuring organizational performance. It defines the proprietary interest of the stakeholders of the enterprise in the balance sheet that declares the resources controlled by the organization, the claims against the resources from creditors and the net interest of the owners. It measures the through-put, the flow of inputs into the production and distribution process and the flow of outputs and revenues, defining over any accounting period, the net incomes accruing to the stakeholders after due allowances for capital consumption during the production period.

If the enterprise paradigm establishes an accounting system that measures revenues, costs and incomes for enterprise owners, the *new community paradigm* must do the same for communities. The shift in viewpoint, from private owner to community and the community's stakeholders, clearly internalizes costs – environmental and social – that escape individual enterprise accounts. This means that this net income measurement is a more accurate reflection of total costs incurred by society in the generation of outputs. The professional managers are trained as agents of the worldview and the valuation logic and as operators of the technology.

The objective is to give substance to an operational model of a community. Enterprise management has developed into a hard-nosed science and art because the concept of enterprise has had the benefit of translation into a clear, unambiguous operating model, with performance standards measured through an elaborate accounting system, and operating protocols embodied in textbooks with principles and cases.

The question: can the concept of a community be similarly substantiated? Two reasons dictate that it should be:

1. Enterprise management excludes responsibility for the ecology. This is the reason economists agonize over the problems of 'externalities' – precisely because the whole of the environmental consequences of business operations are external to the enterprise and must be tortured back into consideration to accommodate environmental costs.

2. An authentic sustainable development program must be designed as a consolidation of sustainable development programs at the level of coherent communities, where responsibilities are clearly defined at each level of organization, managers are trained to implement programs, and accounting systems monitor the performance of the managers.

This implies that the role of *manager* needs to be exercised in the community. What are the implications of that role? It assumes the community to be an 'organization' of particular characteristics. The community system combines the ecological system and the human community, habitat and colony. Thus, the choice of the appropriate unit of organization must integrate its stakeholders, its structure, and its stock of resources. The community is an organism subsisting in a territorial habitat on which it has fashioned a life-support system. It has a territory, a natural resource endowment and a working economy that together define both its needs and its capacity to supply them.

The task of establishing a new world order built on these postulates would be equivalent to a global organizational transformation on a scale equal to the transformations wrought by the enterprise paradigm in the past 50 years. The institutional strategy for the global advocacy of such a system would need certain essential elements:

• A consensus among nations that the global imperatives as defined here would require, first of all, a new covenant among nations, a covenant for planetary survival. The most optimistic expectation for the 1992 UN Conference on Environment and Development (UNCED) was the acceptance of such a consensus and the agreement to such a covenant.

16

- Such a covenant would depend ultimately on all the efforts of organizations at the levels of local communities, villages, towns, metropolitan neighborhoods, whole countries and regions to organize local civil societies and raise their awareness.

- But beyond that, the communities must be helped to become rigorous and disciplined organizations, effectively led, professionally managed, with efficient participatory modes of rational decision making, to the point of being able to register their own valuations and resource-allocating decisions in markets.

- There would be adopted internationally a principle of subsidiarity under which every community seeks the internal development that its members freely choose and finds its own balance with its habitat. The international community is viewed as a community of communities. Inter-community trade seeks to establish patterns that genuinely enhance the respective 'carrying capacities' of the trading communities by offering opportunities for authentic gains after taking into account the full environmental and other costs of the traded products.

- There would be respect for 'infant communities' that desire to achieve a level of internal development and preserve the use of their territories' carrying capacities for the use of their own members first. In the historical development of the countries that were in the group that industrialized before the industrial enterprise giants established their influence, the communities in the municipalities had an opportunity to achieve levels and styles of development that were marked by their own cultural diversities. This was true particularly of the countries that went through a feudal period and then a period of mercantilist protection, particularly at municipal levels. This particular phase in economic evolution is usually only marked for condemnation in histories viewed by the votaries of classical and neoclassical economics.

These essential elements need complementary actions and institutions in order to engineer change. These complementary actions and institutions are within the United Nations, specialized financial institutions, and in the area of trade.

Within the United Nations the complementary actions and institutions would include:

- A strategic rethinking of the United Nations, its mission, the distribution of the responsibilities of its specialized agencies, and the whole organization and culture of the present UN system.

- The elevation of the role of the UN Council for Sustainable Development into a General Assembly function – in the character of a new Planetary Security Council and the redefinition of global security to include the concerns of global sustainability. Planetary survival must become a mainstream concern of the world's governments and civil societies.

- Transformation of the United Nations Development Program (UNDP) into a UN Sustainable Human Development Program (UNSHDP).[21] But redefine the paradigm to center development around the world's communities as the primary units of organization, planning and management. The UNSHDP would carry the primary responsibility for translating community-based sustainable human development into feasible program and project packages.

Within specialized financial institutions, their roles must be redefined to make them the principal mobilizers of resources of this global survival movement. At least three new global institutions will be required: An Inter-Community Sustainable Trade Organization (ICSTO), an Inter-Community Clearing Union (ICCU), and a Sustainable Human Development Bank (SHDB). The mission of the old and new institutions would be to:

- put world-class technological, financial and managerial disciplines to the task of translating community-based sustainable human development into feasible program and project packages;

- develop the technical and financial designs, and the technical and managerial human resources, for communities to plan and manage sustainable development strategies and operational tactics;

- mobilize financial and other resources from the range of multilateral and bilateral, philanthropic and commercial sources to support regional and national programs for community empowerment in the pursuit of sustainable human development.

• facilitate inter-community economic and financial relations and induce free and open trade among communities as a means of genuinely enhancing the sustainable carrying capacities of their respective resources for the benefit and support of the community constituencies.

The third complementary action is in the area of trade. In the present world order, trade is really inter-enterprise exchange. This includes so-called international trade. In fact, the term globalization does not describe the current global trend. Transnationalization is more precise. It defines what is happening to economic activity: it is transcending allegiance to territory. It is becoming a-local and therefore indifferent to any portion of the planet. At the same time, the triple imperative of sustainability – social equity, ecological integrity and economic efficiency – demands that resource management decisions be governed by these considerations as convergent goals.

Agenda 21, the concluding document of UNCED, recognized this as a key problem in achieving sustainable development:

Prevailing systems for decision-making in many countries tend to separate economic, social and environmental factors at the policy, planning and management levels. This influences the actions of all groups in society, including Governments, industry and individuals, and has important implications for the efficiency and sustainability of development. An adjustment or even a fundamental reshaping of decision-making, in light of country-specific conditions, may be necessary if environment and development is to be put at the center of economic and political decision-making, in effect achieving a full integration of these factors.[22]

The objective proposed in *Agenda 21* of improving or restructuring 'the decision-making process so that consideration of socio-economic and environmental issues is fully integrated and a broader public participation assured' sounds fairly straightforward and simple. But on closer examination, carrying it out in practice calls for quite a few fundamental elements.

First, for social, economic and environmental considerations to be integrated at all levels of a participatory decision process, it is necessary to have a conceptual framework that makes it possible to understand the mutual relationships among social, economic and environmental factors. This integration must be understood as a total system if it is to be managed as a total system. But vertical sector-specialization has been a mark of our civilization for at least two hundred years. Our thinking is sector-specialized. This is the 'paradigm' problem.

Second, as is our thinking, so our organizations are also sector-specialized. For decision making to be holistic as the objective requires, organizations must have holistic objectives that combine social and environmental as well as economic performance targets. This is the organization problem.

Third, managements must have operating systems that are holistic, encompassing control systems that relate controlled variables to social, environmental and economic end-results. Further, if decision processes are to be shared, then organizations must be defined in relatively 'flat' rather than steeply hierarchical structures. This is the operating system problem.

Fourth, the performance must be translatable into correspondingly holistic accounting measurement so that managements are able to track their performance. This is the accounting problem.

To address these four problems calls for an institutional strategy that sets in operation, with massive political will and the direct and positive support of national and local governments, a community-centered human development movement that will parallel the current enterprise-centered economic activity at global and national levels. The idea is to empower communities rather than to dis-empower enterprise. But it is important to ensure that the playing field is level, and that governments act as equalizers rather than supporters of enterprise interventions.

Equalization means that real options for an alternative economic organization, and means of sustainable livelihood, are opened up for communities. In addition, communities will be assisted to make conscious decisions about lifestyle and the precise modes they will adopt for achieving the appropriate balance between their traditional values, culture patterns, resource management modes and modernization for enhancing the productivity and carrying capacity of their allotted portions of the earth's resources. It means communities will have the means to enter into their own alliances and mergers with other communities to achieve economies that accrue to their incomes and authentic welfare and improve their respective competitive positions *vis-a-vis* enterprise in the market arena. It means their empowerment to establish at their local levels the functional tension between private gain and community interest.

The vision of sustainable development dictates a new mission and strategy. Community would become the central actor in place of enterprise, and governments would be guided by communitarian philosophy rather than the eighteenth-century atomistic and individualistic liberal philosophy. The fundamental shift in worldview and intellectual framework would demand a corresponding transformation in the organizational structure, operational protocols, staffing and culture of institutions.

A historical analysis of the stages through which enterprise domination became a global reality, and the role of the Bretton Woods institutions in the process, provides valuable insights for detailing the alternative strategy.

The first prerequisite is to flesh out the model of viable, sustainably developing local communities. They must be made as rigorously operational as individual enterprises. They must have distinct legal personalities, clear rights over defined stocks of natural resources delineated in ways that are ecologically meaningful, authority over their territorial jurisdiction, have an operating technology, a career corps of trained managers and a formal accounting system to track the viability of their performance.

Further, they must then have formal criteria for managing their trading and other fiscal and financial relations with the 'citizens' of other communities at successively larger levels in the hierarchy of organizations, building up towards an international network of interrelating communities.

The role of international organizations would be to support this empowerment of communities so that they are the principal actors in the development process. The implications of this shift in perspective are far-reaching.

It requires, first of all, a 'de-sectoralization' of intellectual perspectives, professional specializations and organizational divisions. The unit of sustainable development action is the sustainably developing local community in its local habitat. The hierarchical levels are successively larger communities in correspondingly larger ecological territories.

The fundamental character of these shifts is only appreciated if one realizes the depth, penetration, and all-pervasiveness of sectoral specialization in the ruling economic order and in the international organizations – the UN system, the BWIs, the regional development banks, governments, private-sector business and even in civil society, the academy and the scientific communities.

21

CONCLUSION

The shift toward equitable, sustainable and participatory development requires a whole new culture in which organizations think of sustainable development in terms of whole communities in relation to their respective habitats, rather than in terms of sector-specialized enterprises and capital projects. It demands a whole new discipline to combine in feasibility appraisals, such that social and ecological criteria are integrated with economic criteria. A new breed of managers must emerge that manages communities toward integral goals where economic efficiency is defined to include social equity and ecological wholeness as integral outputs from the use of resources.

Ideas – movements – institutions: these define the sequence and process of social transformation. Ideas become dominant among a critical mass of people and stimulate social movements. Social movements topple old institutions or energize them with a new spirit and a new culture. Such a process established the hegemony of the ruling economic order responsible for the enterprise-centered, growth-obsessed, unsustainable world that we have. It will take a similar process to transform our world into the community-centered sustainable socioeconomic order that alone can save humanity and its habitat.

Notes

1. 'Intellectual paradigm', 'worldview' and 'ideology' have precise meanings. 'Intellectual paradigm' refers to Thomas Kuhn's epistemology and analytical method that forms the basis of a 'school' of scientists for whom the application of the method is 'normal science'. 'Worldview' is *Weltanschauung*, a conception of the universe that forms the basis for a philosophy of life. 'Ideology' has the meaning that Karl Mannheim gives it in *Ideology and Utopia* (1952) and that George C. Lodge describes in his approach to 'ideology analysis'. In *The New American Ideology* (New York, Alfred A. Knopf, 1975, p. 7), Lodge defines an ideology as 'a collection of ideas that makes explicit the nature of the good community ... the framework by which a community defines and applies values, such as survival, justice, self-respect, fulfillment and economy (the efficient use of resources)'. Central to the analysis of this chapter is the process by which a scientific paradigm for understanding reality becomes a universally

adopted worldview and then an ideology according to which reality
is then deliberately transformed.

2. Karl Polanyi, *The Great Transformation* (New York and Toronto:
   Rinehart & Company, Inc., 1944), p. 3.
3. See Paul Kennedy, *The Rise and Fall of the Great Powers: Economic
   Change and Military Conflict from 1500 to 2000* (New York: Random
   House, 1987), p. 4.
4. Polanyi, *The Great Transformation*, chapter 1, 'The Hundred Years'
   Peace'.
5. For example, see Lilian C.A. Knowles, *Economic Development in the
   Nineteenth Century: France, Germany, Russia and the United States*
   (London: Routledge & Sons, 1932), chapter 1.
6. Kennedy, *The Rise and Fall*, p. 143.
7. 'The End of Laissez-Faire' was first published as a pamphlet in July,
   1926 and was based on lectures delivered at Oxford in November
   1924 and Berlin in June 1926. It is reprinted in John Maynard
   Keynes, *Collected Writings, Vol. IX: Essays in Persuasion* (London:
   MacMillan, 1972), pp. 272–4. The 'General Theory' refers to
   Keynes' theoretical demonstration that the free-market economy
   need not establish overall equilibrium at a full employment level.
   This was embodied in his book, the *General Theory of Employment
   Interest and Money*, first published in 1936.
8. Walter Russell Mead, 'American Economic Policy in the Antemillennial Era' in *World Policy Journal*, vol. 6, no. 3, 1989, p. 396.
9. In Keynes' statement before the Commission constituted to study
   the proposed design for the Bank, he explicitly advanced the importance of global development beyond reconstruction. According to
   Seymour Harris (ed.), *The New Economics: Keynes' Influence on
   Theory and Public Policy* (New York: Alfred A. Knopf, 1948) p. 397,
   the Opening Remarks at the First Meeting of the Second Commission on the Bank, July 3, 1944 were:

> It is likely, in my judgement, that the field of reconstruction from
> the consequences of war will mainly occupy the proposed Bank in
> its early days. But as soon as possible, and with increasing
> emphasis as time goes on, there is a second primary duty laid
> upon it, namely, to develop the resources and productive capacity
> of the world, with special attention to the less developed coun-
> tries, to raising the standard of life and the conditions of labor
> everywhere, to make the resources of the world more fully avail-
> able to all mankind, and so to order its operations as to promote
> and maintain equilibrium in the international balances of pay-
> ments of all member countries.

10. Richard Cantillon, *Essai Sur la Nature du Commerce en General*, translation by Henry Higgs, July 1931, (London: MacMillan, 1931). Written by Cantillon between 1730 and 1734, Chapter XIII discusses the particular role of the entrepreneur, translated by Higgs as 'Undertaker', as the person who assumes the venture risk. For example, from pp. 47–49 of Higg's translation:

> The Farmer is an undertaker who promises to pay to the Land-owner, for his Farm or Land, a fixed sum of money (generally supposed to be equal in value to the third of the produce) without assurance of the profit he will derive from this enterprise. He employs part of the land to feed flocks, produce corn, wine, hay, etc. according to his judgment without being able to foresee which of these will pay best.

As quoted in Ronald H. Coase, 'The Nature of the Firm' in Stigler and Boulding (eds), *Readings in Price Theory* (Nashville, TN: American Economic Association, 1952), p. 332, Sir Arthur Salter's description of the economic system is:

> The normal economic system works itself. For its current operation it is under no central control, it needs no central survey. Over the whole range of human activity and human need, supply is adjusted to demand, and production to consumption, by a process that is automatic, elastic and responsive.

The distinction between the allocation of resources in a firm and the allocation in the economic system has been very vividly described by Maurice Dobb when discussing Adam Smith's conception of the capitalist:

> It began to be seen that there was something more important than the relations inside each factory or unit captained by an undertaker; there were the relations of the undertaker with the rest of the economic world outside his immediate sphere ... the undertaker busies himself with the division of labour inside each firm and he plans and organises consciously, but he is related to the much larger economic specialisation, of which he himself is merely one specialised unit. Here he plays his part as a single cell in a larger organism, mainly unconscious of the wider role he fills. (*Capitalist Enterprise and Social Progress*, as quoted in Coase (1952), p. 334.)

11. Adolf A. Berle, Jr and Gardiner C, Means, *The Modern Corporation and Private Property* (New York: MacMillan, 1932), p. 1.
12. Alfred Chandler and Takashi Hikino, *Scale and Scope: The Dynamics of Industrial Capitalism* (Cambridge, MA: The Belknap Press of Harvard University Press, 1990), p. 2.
13. John Kenneth Galbraith, *The New Industrial State* (Boston: Houghton Mifflin Company, 1967), pp. 8–10.
14. Chandler and Hikino, *Scale and Scope*, pp. 608–12.
15. See especially the section, 'The Market Through the Ages', pp. 225–30, in Fernand Braudel, *Civilization and Capitalism, 15th–18th Century: The Wheels of Commerce*, vol. II (New York: Harper & Row, 1982).
16. Robin Broad's account of the evolution of the roles of the IMF and World Bank as major advocates and promoters of what she calls transnationalization in development strategy is adequate to explain the role of the BWIs in shaping the world system according to the neoliberal paradigm. See chapter 2 in particular in Robin Broad, *Unequal Alliance, 1979–1986: The World Bank, the International Monetary Fund, and the Philippines* (Manila: Ateneo de Manila Press, 1988).
17. The term 'ideology' defines what the neoclassical synthesis represented to the world at this time. 'Ideology' is used as a sociological construct, as Karl Mannheim uses it in *Ideology and Utopia* (1952), and as George C. Lodge applied it to the analysis of the fundamental beliefs underlying the American way of life. See George C. Lodge, *The New American Ideology* (1975).
18. See Paul Studenski, *The Income of Nations: Theory, Measurement and Analysis: Past and Present; A Study in Applied Economics and Statistics* (New York: New York University Press, 1958). Studenski's work provides precisely such a comprehensive account of the theory and measurement of national income in different countries, including the translation of Marxist concepts into accounting systems in the Soviet Union. Although national income concepts go back a few centuries and attempts to estimate national income and wealth for different countries go back in England to William Petty in the seventeenth century, the adoption of the concept by governments did not happen until late in the nineteenth century, and the universalization of the practice as an official matter not until after World War II. In this, the propagation of Keynesian economics was definitely a most important factor. Development planning in the Third World after the 1950s and through the 1960s and 1970s was centered on the national accounts as the basis for setting targets and formulating national resource budgets.
19. United Nations Development Programme (UNDP), *Human Development Report 1994* (New York: Oxford University Press, 1994), p. 1.

20. Technology itself is a social construct and its development is a social rather than a deterministic mechanical process; as such, that development is marked by conflict and struggle. See David F. Noble, *Forces of Production: A Social History of Industrial Automation* (New York: Alfred A. Knopf, 1984), pp. 324 ff.

21. James Gustave Speth, Administrator, UNDP, 'Building a New UNDP: Agenda for Change', Presentation before the UNDP Executive Board, February 17, 1994. After recounting all the fundamental changes in the global scene that necessitate a change in UNDP strategy, and taking into account the critique of past Official Development Assistance (ODA) performance, a new role for the UN, and the weaknesses of UNDP itself, he underlines the reasons for the need of UNDP to change (the emphases are Speth's):

a. *in order to become a leading advocate for new approaches to international cooperation for development and for a new ODA*;

b. ... The United Nations has got to be the major force for sustainable human development, for global human security, and for new and reformed methods of international cooperation for development ... *UNDP has got to change in order to help the UN realize this potential.*

c. And finally, *to respond to its identified weaknesses and realize the potential inherent in its mandate.*

Speth calls for a 'new paradigm of sustainable human development' and 'new approaches to development cooperation that achieving sustainable human development will require'. But his definition of sustainable human development falls short of an authentic paradigm shift. He still stays within the enterprise, nation state, and neoclassical frameworks. The Human Development Index is still very much an *ex post* supplement to the national income accounting, which is in essence consolidated enterprise accounting.

22. UNCED Concluding Document, Agenda 21, Section 8.2.

2. Adjusting the Bretton Woods Institutions to Contemporary Realities

Daniel D. Bradlow and Claudio Grossman

INTRODUCTION

The sovereign states that participated in the establishment of the post-World War II international order had a specific vision of how international organizations would function in it. The vision was based on two premises. The first was that the most significant actor in the international order was the sovereign state. Consequently, only states could join and participate in the affairs of the new international organizations, which were themselves constrained in their ability to interfere in the internal affairs of their members.[1] The second premise was that each organization should have a limited mandate to deal with a specific and defined set of problems, with the exception of the United Nations, which has general powers within a constitutional framework.[2] The founding states expected each organization to confine its activities to its specific responsibilities. For example, the International Bank for Reconstruction and Development (IBRD, or 'World Bank') would deal with issues of 'economic development' but would leave monetary questions to the International Monetary Fund (IMF) and health issues to the World Health Organization (WHO).

Since then, the world has undergone such substantial change that the validity of these operating premises has become questionable. The structures of international organizations, based on exclusive state membership, are being challenged by the increasing number of actors on the international scene. The ability of such non-state actors as individuals, corporations, non-governmental organizations

(NGOs), and national liberation movements to influence international affairs has expanded dramatically. Concurrently, the sovereignty of states has declined in the sense that they have a diminished ability to manage problems within their borders. This means that most problems can be solved only through collaborative efforts involving state, non-state and international actors. The effective functioning of international organizations with limited mandates has also been compromised by the growing complexity of the problems they face. In particular, clear jurisdictional boundaries between international organizations have become blurred as world problems have become more intricate and intertwined.

International organizations have failed to respond adequately to these challenges. Their decision-making bodies and operating rules are still premised on the exclusivity of the sovereign state's role. Furthermore, they have not developed effective mechanisms for co-ordinating policies and operations in areas where their activities extend into the jurisdiction of other organizations. The result is that most international organizations are seeking to solve current problems with institutional arrangements designed for a bygone era.

The international organizations that have been most forcefully confronted with the difficulties posed by these changes are the IMF and the World Bank Group, or collectively, the Bretton Woods institutions (BWIs). This chapter studies the BWIs and the changes they must make in order to respond to today's challenges. The first and second parts of the chapter discuss the developments that are shaping the world in which the BWIs must operate. The third part assesses the challenges facing them and the responses they have made thus far. The last section will propose some specific actions the BWIs could take in order to react effectively to the exigencies of the modern world.

DEVELOPMENTS THAT HAVE PRODUCED INTERTWINED PROBLEMS

Defining the Issues

It is a truism that all human problems are related to each other. However, it is also true that the possibility of solving them is substantially diminished if they are all treated as integrally related. For this reason, international organizations were given specific and limited mandates, with the jurisdiction of each organization circumscribed so that it dealt only with a prescribed set of issues. They were also limited to dealing with only those aspects of their issues that have international implications. Accordingly, different international organizations were created to deal with different sets of problems, such as peace, security, health, agriculture, global capital flows for development, management of exchange rates and international trade.

Since the end of World War II, there has been a steady increase in the number of issues whose effects spill over national boundaries, and which states are unable to solve, or even manage, in isolation. Examples of these issues are poverty; refugees; environmental degradation; nuclear proliferation; financial flows; transfers of technology; the effect of globalized production patterns on taxes, trade, labor and consumers, and criminal law problems such as drug and arms trafficking.

The increase of internationalized problems has highlighted how intertwined these problems are, in the sense that it has become more difficult to resolve any one problem in isolation from the others. Thus, the BWIs cannot address problems of poverty without considering issues of refugees, environmental degradation, population policy, the capacity of the state to manage its resources, and human rights (including the status of women, indigenous people and minorities). Environmentalists cannot seek resolution of environmental problems without addressing issues of poverty, refugees, information flows, population and even security. Trade organizations can no longer effectively regulate trade without addressing environmental issues, labor policy, investment matters, intellectual property (which itself raises important cultural rights issues) and trade in services (which raises additional important monetary, financial and immigration policy questions). Human rights organizations cannot seek effective protection of human rights without considering the impact of poverty, foreign investment, trade and environmental degradation on them.

The multitude of connections between these problems has broken down the forced distinction that the international community sought to maintain between purely domestic and purely international problems.[3] Almost all issues now have both domestic and international dimensions to them. Proper resolution to each problem, therefore, requires coordinated action on local, regional and global levels.

Background on International Organizations

The international organizations established after World War II were organized around the principle of sovereignty, which meant that only nations were eligible for membership. Only member states had (and still have) a vote in the policymaking bodies of these organizations. Non-state actors who wished to participate had to present their views through their state representatives.[4] In accordance with the principles of sovereignty, international organizations had only limited power to intervene in the 'internal affairs' of their member states.[5] This also reflected the fact that the international community was more interested in using these organizations to promote global peace and cooperation than as a mechanism for enforcing state compliance with international standards of conduct.[6]

The most important international organizations created after World War II were the United Nations, the IMF and the IBRD (World Bank). The United Nations was granted a broad mandate. The Security Council has authority to deal with threats to the peace, breaches of the peace and acts of aggression. The General Assembly has the power to discuss any issue within the scope of the UN Charter, which encompasses issues ranging from human rights to international economic relations to peace and security. The IMF was mandated to regulate a monetary order based on its members' commitment to freely convertible currencies and stable exchange rates. The World Bank was originally established to fund the reconstruction of war-torn Europe and the development of the poorer countries of the world. Its mandate was to facilitate the investment of capital for production purposes and encourage development of member-countries' production facilities.

Though organized around the principle of sovereignty, in reality, the United Nations and the BWIs constitute a movement away from an international legal order based on absolute sovereignty. The charters of both the United Nations and the IMF create a superstructure that operates above the individual member states. Each state agrees to surrender aspects of its sovereignty in return for the political, economic and security benefits they expect to derive from membership.

On joining the United Nations, states agree to limit their use of force, submit to Security Council decisions relating to international peace and security, and accept the General Assembly's broad authority to discuss publicly issues of international concern. The benefits that states expected to derive from the United Nations have been constrained by problems beyond its control. The Cold War severely limited the Security Council's ability to take action on threats to peace, and serious differences of opinion between the richest countries and the developing countries have hindered the United Nations' ability to act in the international economic arena. However, these deficiencies should not be inter-

preted as meaning that the United Nations has always been ineffective. It has provided a forum for discussion and initiation of
action on many relevant issues facing the international community. In human rights, environmental, and decolonization cases,
the United Nations has played an essential role in establishing
entitlements and standards of conduct, and providing supervisory
mechanisms that promoted state compliance with these standards
and respect for these entitlements.[7] This has been achieved
through the organization's interpretation of the concept of 'domestic jurisdiction'. Early in its history, the United Nations determined that the requirement that it not intervene in the domestic
jurisdiction of its member states did not prevent it from debating
and issuing recommendations on issues of interest and concern.
The most outstanding example of this creative use of its authority
is the United Nations' treatment of the issue of apartheid.[8]

Similarly, by joining the IMF, states agree to surrender some
control over their exchange rate and monetary policy. In return,
they expect to benefit from the establishment of international
monetary rules that the IMF, through regular consultations with
its member countries, can monitor and enforce.[9] Perceived benefits include opportunities for economic growth and financial support from the IMF if the country experiences difficulty in meeting
its international monetary obligations. Membership in the IMF
also entitles states to join the World Bank, where poorer countries
can obtain financing for development projects, and richer countries can benefit from the business opportunities created by the
Bank's lending operations.[10] World Bank loans, which necessarily
entail the imposition of conditions on borrowing countries, also
contribute to the erosion of absolute sovereignty.[11]

The decision to grant the BWIs limited supervision over members' activities has proven remarkably dynamic. Over the past 50
years, the BWIs have steadily increased both their involvement in
the affairs of member countries and their ability to exercise
supervision over them. However, this development has been mani-
festly uneven. Today the BWIs exercise substantial control over
the affairs of poorer member countries, but have very little power
over the richer ones.[12]

Over time, the IMF has assumed more responsibility for con-
fronting the structural economic problems of developing member
countries,[13] which forces those countries to deal with some of
their developmental, as opposed to monetary, problems. However,
the IMF does not pay adequate attention to the social impact of
its policies.[14]

The Bank has undergone an even more dramatic transformation.

Confronted by the developmental problems of borrower countries, and by the failure of many Bank-funded projects to perform as expected, the Bank has shifted its focus from an exclusive concern with discrete development projects to a regard for the general policy environment within which the project must function. Accordingly, the Bank, in addition to its project lending operations, has begun to provide loans for general adjustments, so-called structural adjustment loans (SALs), and for sector-specific adjustments, so-called sectoral adjustment loans (SECALs), conditional on certain policy reforms. The conditions, which are contractually binding obligations, involve the adoption of institutional or legislative measures intended to 'adjust' the structures within which economic activity occurs or economic and social policy is made. The measures are taken to encourage economic growth, but they are capable of producing unforeseen and unwanted side-effects.[15]

This shift in the focus of Bank operations has forced it to address explicitly the institutional constraints that influence the borrower's ability to implement and sustain policy reforms. In so doing, the Bank has incorporated into its loan agreements conditions relating to those aspects of governance that influence a country's capacity to formulate and implement policies. This means that, in fact, the Bank through its loan negotiations and ongoing dialogue with borrower states, has become an active participant in their policymaking processes, influencing the form and substance of their policies.[16]

The evolution of these international organizations' mandates, which has involved them in what were once considered purely internal matters, has perforce undermined the concept of states' sovereignty. It has also compelled them to become more receptive to demands by private actors for increased public participation in their affairs.[17] In addition, the BWIs need to reformulate their operating procedures and responsibilities, and to modify their relations with other international organizations, to make them more appropriate to their evolving functions. Some proposals for this are discussed in the last section of this chapter.

The New International Actors

The complexities created by intertwined problems and solutions are compounded by a dramatic increase in the number of actors on the international stage. Business organizations, national liberation movements, political parties, trade unions, individuals and NGOs[18] have all become significant players on the international stage. They are developing transnational affiliations and the ability to operate internationally, which means that they can effectively advocate their interests at the international level.

The most significant example of this phenomenon is the rise of the transnational corporation (TNC). While TNCs have existed for centuries, the scope of their influence and operations has grown dramatically as the post-World War II era has unfolded. Stimulated by new investment opportunities and technological developments, TNCs now produce goods and services in multiple locations, encouraging global production and distribution patterns, and global strategic planning. However, the fact that TNCs have multiple production facilities means that they also have increased their ability to evade state power and undermine the efficacy of national regulatory schemes by moving operations among their facilities around the world. This growth in corporate power poses problems for the international community. First, it means that, whatever the legal status of the state, it has lost power to TNCs in terms of control over human, natural, financial and other resources.[19] It also means that the private actors – trade unions, consumer groups, environmental organizations – that traditionally have interacted with TNCs on a country-by-country basis must now transnationalize so that they can interact meaningfully with TNCs.

The growing influence of TNCs and other non-state actors also affects international organizations. Like the state, they now cannot effectively perform their functions or implement their mandates without the support and participation of relevant non-state actors.

FORCES FOR CHANGE

Recent developments have dramatically increased pressure on the BWIs to respond to the growing number of international actors, intertwined problems, and the resulting decrease in the sovereign power of member states. In particular, there are four historical forces challenging the BWIs:

1. technological changes facilitating the creation of a global economy and global society;

2. development of international human rights law;

3. increasing concern in the international community about the environment; and

4. changing perceptions of peace and security.

These developments and their implications for the BWIs are discussed in the following section.

Technological Changes

In the past 15 to 20 years, developments in information technologies and telecommunications have revolutionized the world economy and the way people conduct their day-to-day affairs. Technology is 'globalizing' the international economy and creating transnational linkages between private actors. Investors can use computer programs to plan investment strategies, and electronic transfers to instantaneously move their funds around the world in search of the best returns. Engineers who work for the same company, but in different countries, can use computer technology to work together on the same design project. Researchers and scholars located around the world can conduct ongoing dialogues over electronic mail (e-mail) networks. Human rights and other social activists can use faxes and e-mail to inform the world of developments in their countries, and the media can then spread this information virtually instantaneously around the world.[20]

While these technological developments open up exciting possibilities for human development, it should be recognized that they significantly diminish state sovereignty. Many activities now take place at speeds that make it difficult for state regulators to detect them in advance. Regulators may also find it virtually impossible to trace a completed action or to identify the actor. In addition, relatively easy access to the computers and networks that are the infrastructure for these new technologies makes it difficult for states to regulate their use. In fact, those states that have sought to limit the public's access or their right to use these technologies have found that the price, in terms of their ability to participate in the international economy, is higher than they wish to pay.[21]

The result is that these technologies empower private actors to neutralize the regulatory efforts of their sovereign government and even, in some cases, to undermine its legitimacy and authority. Moreover, they enable individuals and groups to develop connections to individuals and groups outside the state that can be stronger than those to their compatriots. This could result in the weakening of national consciousness and the inchoate beginnings of a global consciousness.

In such an environment, the efficacy of international organizations allowing only state participation is open to serious question.

Corporations, industry associations, NGOs and other private actors play too active a role in international affairs to be excluded from participation in international organizations. New technologies have so enhanced the power of private actors relative to the state that it is often not feasible to establish sustainable international or domestic standards of conduct without their participation.[22]

Human Rights

Since the adoption of the Universal Declaration of Human Rights in 1948,[23] the international human rights system has undergone substantial evolution. The Universal Declaration has acquired legal force either as an instrument of interpretation of the UN Charter or as part of customary law. In addition, the international community's efforts to establish universally applicable standards of conduct has resulted in the adoption of numerous human rights treaties. The international community has also embarked on the supervision of compliance by signatories to these treaties.[24] These developments have created unprecedented opportunity for individuals to seek international protection against their own governments. A substantial international human rights jurisprudence has emerged, accompanied by a broadening of the dialogue on human rights to include private actors,[25] and the formulation of new 'third generation' rights.[26]

Notwithstanding these impressive advances in human rights, much remains to be done in the areas of prevention and enforcement. Early warning mechanisms and a culture of human rights must be more fully developed and implemented. The fact that victims cannot be confident that they will obtain redress has been dramatically demonstrated by the international community's inability to deal with human rights tragedies in Bosnia and Rwanda. In addition to social, economic and cultural rights, the rights of women, children and indigenous peoples are still not adequately recognized in practice. The law also remains undeveloped in regard to such complex third generation rights as the right to development and the right to a clean environment. Despite these shortcomings, it is clear that the evolution of the human rights system has been sufficient to inject these considerations into the making of environmental and development policy, and even into the allocation of international development assistance.

The connection between development and human rights[27] obliges the BWIs to address the issue of how to incorporate human rights considerations into their operations. This raises a number of complex issues, the first being that the charters and operating principles of the BWIs place limits on their ability to take political considerations into account. However, the inevitable impact of BWI decisions on human rights makes it difficult for them to avoid consideration of at least some political issues without impairing their efficacy. The attempt to resolve the conflict between their limited mandates and the need to adequately account for the human rights impact of their work has resulted in the BWIs having to use standard economic arguments to justify actions that are, in fact, premised on human rights. For example, the World Bank and the IMF recently won a commitment from Burkina Faso to combat female genital mutilation as part of its Policy Framework Paper. They reasoned that this issue fell within their mandate because female genital mutilation increases the risks of maternal death at childbirth and of still-births, both of which have obvious adverse economic effects.

It should be noted that their failure to address human rights issues in a forthright manner has meant that the BWIs have not effectively incorporated human rights into their policies and operations. A good example is that the BWIs have recognized the importance of participation to successful sustainable development, but have failed to condition their funds on the borrower-state's respect for the freedoms of association and speech. They have also been unable to develop a plan for responding to a borrower-state's repression of groups that, having accepted the BWIs' offer to express their opinions, advance positions antagonistic to the state. Furthermore, the BWIs have not felt compelled to follow the recommendations and decisions of other international organizations with greater experience in this area.[28]

Another aspect of human rights that is relevant to the work of the BWIs arises from the debate about the existence of a hierarchy of human rights.[29] The international community treats all human rights as being of equal status. Current human rights law does not give states or international organizations clear guidance on the proper sequencing of human rights in a sustainable development plan. Furthermore, there is no international consensus on how to translate human rights principles into a human rights-sensitive, sustainable development program.

These deficiencies in the policies and operations of the BWIs were not important as long as it was practical for each of them to focus only on its own area of specialization. The intertwined nature of human rights, development and environmental issues, and the BWIs' increasing policymaking role, have made these deficiencies less tolerable. Thus, given their limited mandates, the BWIs, working in cooperation with other international organiza-

tions, must devise the means for assessing the human rights implications of their policies and operations.

Environmental Concerns

The recognition that the global environment cannot absorb all the
waste created by the international economy, and that this limitation imposes a relatively fixed constraint on economic growth, has
profound implications. Until recently, scholars and policymakers
analyzed human activity in terms of how people arranged themselves for the production and distribution of the goods and services needed for individual and social well-being. The recognition of
environmental constraints is forcing them to shift their attention
to the process of consumption.[30]
Virtually all human activity can be viewed as consuming the
earth's environment. Policymakers and scholars must account for
the costs of this consumption if they are to accurately assess the
environmental and social repercussions of the specific activity, as
well as its economic consequences. This means that questions
must be asked both about the present direct and indirect effects
of our activities and about their impact on intergenerational
equity. All costs must be internalized and accounted for in the
planning process, including not just the costs of actual consumption, but also 'consumption opportunity costs' (that is, the cost of
forgoing alternative consumption opportunities).
This paradigmatic shift exposes the connections between the
economic issues that the BWIs were created to address and other
aspects of human existence. For example, inadequate environmental assessments can distort the financial and economic analysis of
particular projects and programs, thereby leading the BWIs to
fund unsustainable development projects. In addition, the BWIs
have learned that effective environmental analysis requires an
understanding of the social impact of proposed operations. Thus,
adequate environmental analyses requires public participation.[31]
Productive public participation, in turn, is only possible if there
are unhindered information flows to the public. Thus, the incorpo-
ration of environmental issues into the work of the BWIs has led
them to address important human rights issues such as freedom of
speech and association, academic freedom and access to political
and legal processes. It also raises questions about the efficacy of
the hierarchical institutional arrangements of the BWIs. Their
present bureaucratic structures are not well suited to planning and
executing operations that emphasize public participation and the

free flow of information.[32] These operations require structures that can encourage and respond to actions initiated from the broad base of stakeholders in the operation rather than structures that rely on actions being initiated from the senior levels of their own and their borrowers' institutions.

The international community's recognition of the importance of the environment to the BWIs' operations has also resulted in an increase in the number of parties who have a stake in and wish to participate in the formulation and implementation of their operations. BWI stakeholders now include those non-governmental environmental organizations who want to have a say in those international organizations whose operations affect the global environment. Moreover, because of the opportunities created by new technologies, they have the knowledge, power and international connections to make their presence felt.

The failure of the BWIs to incorporate fully and effectively these private actors as well as all other stakeholders into their work deprives them of an important source of expertise and information. It also could result in the BWIs adopting policies and standards that are opposed by those most directly affected by these operations. It also creates the impression that the BWIs are undermining democracy by supporting unrepresentative governments in their member states.

Environmental issues, therefore, pose an important challenge to the BWIs. The challenge comes not only from our evolving understanding of the relationship between environment and development, but also from the number of actors interested in BWI activities.

Peace and Security

As the world has become more integrated, the range of factors that influence national and international peace and security has expanded. Threats to well-being can arise from environmental, social and economic sources as well as from traditional military sources. For example, social conflict, caused by environmental degradation in one area, can interrupt the supply of goods and services across the globe. It can cause human migrations that overtax the resources of other countries and turn local conflicts into global ones. In addition, global communication has so enhanced general awareness of the intertwined nature of human problems that the international community has taken a growing interest in conflicts that arguably directly affect only the internal peace of one country.[33]

Given these developments, and fueled by the end of the Cold

War, the international community has begun to recognize that it has an interest in playing a more active role in the promotion of peace and security within nation states as well as globally. It has also begun to acknowledge that keeping the peace involves resolving the *causes* of conflict in addition to dealing with its *manifestations*. The most significant examples of these developments are UN operations in Namibia and Cambodia. In both cases, the United Nations performed many traditional sovereign functions, such as the maintenance of law and order, the organization of elections and the provision of key governmental functions during the period of transition from conflict to peace.

The inadequacy of the international community's response to conflicts in Angola, Bosnia, Haiti and Rwanda suggests that it has not yet been able to define the scope of its obligation to intervene. These examples demonstrate that the international community is not yet ready to accept all the political and financial consequences of this complex form of peacekeeping. It has also not been willing to establish a uniformly applicable set of rules for intervention in the internal affairs of states and social groupings. Nevertheless, these cases confirm that there are powerful forces pushing the international community toward the acceptance of a new reality.

Those cases in which the international community has been willing to undertake complex peacekeeping operations involving the assumption of certain governmental functions raise important considerations of responsibility and accountability. Participants in these international operations are perforce entering into the same relationship to private actors as that usually maintained between national governments and private actors. This suggests that these international peacekeepers have the same responsibilities to private actors as a functioning national government would have. In addition, it suggests that the international community needs to develop suitable means to monitor their behavior.

These developments are affecting the operation of the BWIs. They are being forced to pay closer attention to the level of military expenditures in borrower states. They also must address the issue of the responsibilities of international financial organizations in cases of famine and disaster relief. They are also being forced to recognize that their operations can adversely affect the refugee situation and the level of security in borrower states.

THE CHALLENGE FOR THE BRETTON WOODS INSTITUTIONS

The intertwining of problems has forced the BWIs to broaden their interpretation of their mandates. This expansion has caused a *de facto* blurring of the division between their mandates and those of other international organizations. Moreover, it has made the BWIs players in the policymaking processes of the borrowing member countries.

The World Bank is engaged in a broad policy dialogue with its borrower countries. Since the Bank now makes policy-based loans as well as project loans, these dialogues cover many aspects of the member-country's proposed development plans and its ability to implement these plans. Through this dialogue, the Bank is able to influence a country's policies. This influence is enhanced through the Bank's lending decisions and enforced through the terms and conditions the Bank incorporates into its loan agreements. The result is that the Bank plays a role in both the formulation and the implementation of policies and priorities in borrower countries. This role creates both the potential for and the need to engage in dialogue with the non-governmental actors who will be affected by the policies that the Bank helps formulate.

The IMF conducts broad surveillance missions in member countries. During the course of these missions the IMF and the state discuss aspects of policies relevant to the IMF's mandate of managing the international monetary system and maintaining a stable balance of payments. Monetary and exchange-rate policies affect and are affected by all aspects of an economy. Therefore, in addition to macroeconomic issues, these discussions are likely to include trade, social, fiscal, banking, environmental, labor and military issues and policies.[34] These discussions influence IMF recommendations to the country, the conditions it incorporates into stand-by arrangements, and other mechanisms used to provide financial support.

It should be noted that both the IMF and the Bank are careful to respect the sovereignty of their member states. Consequently, regardless of how policies are developed, it is the borrowers, not the BWIs, who are *legally* responsible for the design and implementation of these policies. The formal legal situation should not, however, be confused with the *functional* reality that the BWIs play an important role in the policymaking process of some of their member states.[35] It should also not be used to allow the BWIs to escape responsibility for the consequences of their actions in this process.

It is important to recognize that the BWIs are capable of exercising this power and influence only over those member countries that make use of their financing services. This means that their power is exercised over the poorer and weaker member countries, which makes it imperative that those affected have a means of holding the BWIs accountable for the consequences of their actions.[36]

The BWIs and Participation

Their policymaking role poses two challenges for the BWIs. First, how can they give all affected parties a voice in policymaking? Second, how can the affected parties hold the BWIs accountable?

Those who play a role in making and implementing a state's development policy assume certain international legal responsibilities. These are determined partly by the treaties the state has signed, and partly by general principles of international law binding on all international actors. Therefore, the BWIs cannot provide funds to countries that are practicing genocide or promoting racial discrimination. Furthermore, international organizations must not advocate policies that would result in member states being forced to violate freely assumed international legal commitments. They also should not provide funding in a way that undermines the member-state's ability to abide by its international commitments. This is particularly pertinent in the case of environmental and human rights agreements.[37]

The principles of international human rights law imply that the BWIs have an obligation to ensure that their operating procedures are open to participation by those non-state actors who have a stake in these operations. The level of participation may vary, depending on the character of the specific BWI operation and the nature of the borrower-state's decision-making processes. However, to guarantee that they satisfy international legal obligations, the BWIs need to develop formal, transparent mechanisms that will assure a minimum level of participation in their operations. These mechanisms can include whatever fora and techniques are appropriate for gathering information and opinions from the stakeholders in the BWIs' operations.[38]

In addition, the BWIs should design a mechanism that, when necessary, allows for participation in their operations by those precluded from taking part in the borrower-state's policymaking process. Those who are unable to take advantage of existing opportunities for participation because they fear retribution from more powerful actors should also be included. The BWIs could establish a mechanism that allows affected people to submit information to them in confidence, or they could allow representatives of those affected by a BWI operation to formally present information on their behalf.

The BWIs and Policymaking

There are two dimensions to BWI responsibilities at the policymaking level. The first is making substantive economic and social policies. Since these policies determine the types of activities funded and their design and implementation, non-state stakeholders have an obvious interest in participating in the substantive policymaking process. At present, the BWIs informally consult interested parties on proposed policies. However, this process is *ad hoc* and not open to all affected parties. A more formal process would ensure that stakeholders have a fair and meaningful opportunity to participate in BWI policymaking. The BWIs can meet this need by creating formal access points where private actors are assured the right to participate. These could include formal, timely invitations from the Bank and the IMF to stakeholders asking for information and proposals on any issue currently under policy review. After the BWIs have had opportunity to consider these submissions, they could prepare a draft version of the policy that would be submitted for public comment. A finalized policy statement that includes a discussion of the comments received by the BWIs should then be published.

An additional method for introducing non-state views into the policymaking procedures of the World Bank would be to revive the International Bank for Reconstruction and Development's Advisory Council. It is possible to expand this council to include representatives of developmental, environmental, women's and human rights organizations.[39] The IBRD's Articles of Agreement stipulate that in fields where specialized international organizations exist, the Bank, in consultation with the relevant specialized agency, shall select Advisory Council representatives who are expert in these areas. The Council's mandate is to 'advise the Bank on matters of general policy'. While it has only advisory powers, it could serve a useful function by publicizing its findings and recommendations. This should help stimulate public debate on the Bank's existing and proposed policies.

Article V(6)(a) states that the Council shall meet annually 'and on such other occasions as the Bank may request'. There is no reason that the Bank could not request the Council to hold regular meetings more often. In addition, the Council could establish specialized sub-committees that would hold regular and frequent meetings on their issues.

The second dimension to BWI responsibilities at policy level relates to the process of formulating the internal operating rules and procedures that guide staff actions. These rules influence all aspects of BWI operations, but they are developed, implemented and interpreted without any formal procedures through which outside actors can influence their content or interpretation. The lack of transparency in this process runs counter to the principles of good governance advocated by the Bank. Therefore, the process should be opened up to greater public participation. This can be done by adopting the same notice-and-comment procedure described for incorporating public participation into substantive policymaking in the Bank.

It should be noted that the Bank's policymaking role is complicated by its Articles of Agreement, which preclude it from intervening in the 'political affairs' of member countries or from being influenced by the 'political character' of member states.[40] The Bank may take only 'economic considerations' into account in its decision making. In point of fact, the Bank, throughout its history, has interpreted and reinterpreted the meaning of 'economic considerations'. With each new interpretation, the Bank has expanded the scope of this term and, concurrently, narrowed the scope of the political prohibition established by Article IV(10).[41] Formerly, the Bank primarily funded discrete infrastructure projects; now it lends money for endeavors such as the reform of a country's judiciary and public sector. These activities suggest that the Bank has been broadening the range of political and human rights issues that it views as falling within its mandate.

While these developments are to be welcomed, they are not sufficient. The Bank uses this creative interpretation in an *ad hoc* manner. Thus it is able to assert that it has authority to address those human rights issues it wishes to confront, such as female genital mutilation and non-state actor participation meanwhile the Bank argues that it does not have the authority to address other major human rights issues, such as the torture of prisoners or the suppression of political dissent, because they are 'political' issues that do not have a 'direct' economic effect.[42] The arbitrariness of these decisions becomes clear when one takes into account the well-documented connections between a free press and hunger; and between free speech, transparent and accountable governance and economic development.

The Bank needs to develop a consistent and thoughtful interpretation of the political prohibition in its charter, and a better understanding of the relationship between human rights, govern-ance and development. In addition, now that it has accepted the importance of participation to sustainable development, it has an obligation to protect those who suffer human rights violations as a result of their participation in the Bank's operations.

The IMF operates under a similar constraint. Article IV(3)(b) of its Articles of Agreement states that the IMF shall 'respect the political and social policies' of its member states. While the IMF interprets this as precluding it from interfering in its member states' domestic political affairs, it has expanded the scope of issues it is willing to address in its consultations with its member states and in the conditions it attaches to its financing arrange-ments. These now include social safety nets for the poor and levels of military expenditures. The IMF has not yet publicly articulated how it distinguishes between those issues which are reasonably within its mandate and those which are purely within the scope of its members domestic political affairs (and therefore outside of the IMF's mandate).

The BWIs and Accountability

The BWIs, through their policymaking functions, directly affect the lives of many individuals. Those affected must be provided with the means to hold the BWIs accountable for their role in the design and implementation of specific operations. The recently established World Bank Inspection Panel presents a useful model for the IMF and the other multilateral development banks in this respect.

The Inspection Panel reviews and investigates complaints from a group of two or more who claim that they have been harmed by the failure of the Bank to comply with its operational rules and policies. Its powers are advisory and investigatory. In all cases, final decision-making power resides with the Bank's executive directors. However, the Bank is required to make all complaints, findings and recom-mendations of the Panel and subsequent decisions publicly avail-able. In addition, the Panel is required to publish an annual report. Thus, even though it has limited powers and jurisdiction, it has the ability to influence the Bank's operational rules and policies, and thereby its operations. Over time, it may also affect the procedures used in formulating Bank operating rules and procedures.[43]

Relations Between the IMF and the World Bank

The expanding operations of the Bank and the IMF have resulted in an overlapping of their respective mandates. This has caused more systematic interactions between the two organizations.[44] The most obvious manifestation of this development is the Policy Framework Paper, which is prepared by borrower countries eligible for funding from the IMF's Enhanced Structural Adjustment Facility (ESAF). It is only adopted after both the IMF and the Bank find the document acceptable. The policies spelled out in this document are the basis on which the IMF provides funds from the ESAF to the country. It may also provide the basis for loans from the World Bank's concessional window, the International Development Association (IDA).

The establishment of the Policy Framework Paper process has reduced the risk of a borrower country being given conflicting advice by the IMF and the Bank. It has also helped streamline negotiations with the BWIs. However, the process tends to limit the country's negotiating power. Whereas previously the country may have had some ability to play one institution against the other, thus expanding its policymaking and funding influence, it is now presented with a united front. Given the fact that other funding sources often take their lead from the BWIs,[45] this coordination can substantially reduce a borrower country's options.

Relations With Other International Organizations

The progressive broadening of BWI operations has resulted in their encroachment into the areas of other international organizations. This necessitates a rethinking of relations, particularly between the BWIs and other specialized agencies in the UN and regional systems.

The Relationship Agreement between the BWIs and the United Nations, while acknowledging that the BWIs are specialized agencies of the United Nations, requires them only to 'consider' UN decisions and recommendations.[46] The BWIs have interpreted these agreements as not requiring them to follow the decisions and recommendations of the United Nations.[47] While this interpretation is not universally accepted, the BWIs continue to contend that they have complete discretion in deciding whether or not to comply with UN decisions. The BWIs are also obliged to give 'due consideration' to the UN's request that items it proposes be placed on the agenda for their Board of Governors meetings.

In addition, they are required to exchange information, special reports and publications 'to the fullest extent practicable'. This is subject to the need for the organizations to 'safeguard' confidential information, and each organization is free to decide what information to withhold from the other.

Over the years, the BWIs have jealously guarded their independence from the United Nations. They have interpreted the Relationship Agreement as granting them, in effect, independent decision-making power on all issues, and as precluding the United Nations from demanding any particular action from them.[48] One consequence of this has been that the BWIs, feeling free to reject the recommendations and decisions of other specialized agencies and of the United Nations itself, have often developed their policies in relative isolation. With the broadening range of BWI activity, the number of areas in which this is occurring has increased to include security, environment, and some human rights, educational and cultural issues.[49]

In principle, the BWIs can make one of two responses whenever their operations encroach on the jurisdiction of other international organizations. The first is to develop their own in-house expertise to deal with these issues. The Bank appears to have adopted this response in the environmental area. The second would be to formally commit to respect and follow the decisions of those international organizations that have specific expertise in the relevant area. While there is no legal requirement to adopt the recommendations or follow the policy guidance of other specialized organizations, the BWIs could publicly pledge to give them serious consideration. Though they have never explicitly adopted this approach, they do engage in dialogue with other international agencies and occasionally change their policies in response. For example, the IMF made some changes in its conditionality policies in light of a United Nations International Children's Emergency Fund (UNICEF) study on adjustment, and the World Bank consults with the WHO on health issues.[50] This is, however, done on an *ad hoc* basis, at the discretion of the BWIs. The second response would be more consistent with a world order in which international organizations, despite the broadening scope of their activities, remain limited to clearly defined mandates. It would also help avoid conflicting policies and unnecessary duplication of effort and expense.

A number of potential problems arise with this alternative. The first is a problem of jurisdiction: there may be more than one relevant organization. Both a global and a regional organization may deal with the issue under consideration, and two agencies acting in the same area may not give consistent guidance to the BWIs. This problem is compounded by the lack of an efficient mechanism for resolving jurisdictional or policy disputes. In addition, other agencies' decisions and recommendations may be difficult to translate into the operationally useful standards needed by the BWIs.

The second problem concerns the competence of the relevant organization: it may not be effective in performing its own mandate and, as a result, the BWIs may lack confidence in its decisions and recommendations. A third potential problem is the danger inherent in centralization: this approach might lead to the Policy Framework Paper 'problem', in the sense that all germane organizations will begin adopting closely coordinated policies. An international orthodoxy on each issue will then be generated that can limit the policy options available to individual countries.

These problems are not insurmountable. To limit the dangers of both anarchic and overly centralized approaches, the BWIs and other international organizations need to strengthen their cooperation, thus avoiding the problems created by BWI encroachment into the jurisdiction of other international organizations.[51] The first step both sets of organizations should take is to improve communications. This would involve extensive and formalized exchanges of information, ideas and expertise among the staffs of the appropriate organizations.[52] A structured program of continuous dialogue on issues of mutual concern should be included. Staff training programs and inter-staff discussions should include exchanges on the findings and recommendations of other international organizations, and should be supplemented by country and thematic reports that incorporate mutually useful information. Both sets of organizations should involve non-governmental actors in their dialogue, training and staff exchange programs. In some cases, particularly in the environmental area, this process is well underway. However, in the human rights area, inter-organizational dialogue is only tentatively beginning.

The increasing encroachment of the BWIs into the work of other international organizations requires them to reassess their obligations under general principles of international law. They need to acknowledge evolving trends in international law and to make explicit their interpretation of its applicability to them. For example, in light of current international concern with democratization and good governance, the BWIs should explicitly state what they consider their obligations to be in promoting such policies as freedom of speech and association.

A PROGRAM OF ACTION

The challenges faced by the BWIs are complex and will not be easily resolved. A successful strategy will require the participation of all stakeholders in their work. The ability to devise an effective response to these challenges is affected by the fact that knowledge and understanding of the issues is still rudimentary. A successful strategy for environmentally sustainable development has not yet emerged. Neither has an operationally useful theory concerning the indivisibility of civil, political, economic, social and cultural rights and its implications for the development process. In addition, those institutional characteristics that would be most effective in dealing with the full range of intertwined problems have not been fully identified. Notwithstanding the need for a comprehensive approach, it is possible to formulate a set of institutional reforms that the BWIs should adopt.

The BWIs need to reinterpret their charters to clarify what issues they consider as outside their mandates. While the political prohibition has continuing validity, it should not prevent the BWIs from incorporating matters governed by international law, such as human rights and environmental protection, into their operation. Such a reinterpretation would facilitate efforts to promote a development process governed by the rule of law.

They should also reinterpret their Relationship Agreements with the United Nations. The BWIs should realize that it is consistent with the terms of these agreements to publicly commit to comply with decisions of the United Nations and its specialized agencies.[53] Similarly, recommendations of regional organizations should be broadly and publicly debated. In those cases where compliance is not possible, the BWIs should publicly explain their decisions.

Information should be collected on their member-states' international legal commitments. In so doing, the BWIs should not limit themselves to the information provided by the state, but should also consult NGOs and other private actors. The BWIs can use the terms and conditions attached to their funding arrangements to achieve this end. For example, the World Bank could make it a condition of their loans and the IMF of their stand-by arrangements that the borrower state provide information on all pertinent international agreements to which it is party, on its interpretation of its obligations under these agreements, and on the measures it has taken or intends to take to comply with them.[54] The BWIs could also demand copies of all reports the borrower state makes, particularly to other international organizations, in connection with these treaty obligations. They should then use this information to ensure that they only fund projects and policies that are in compliance with validly assumed international obligations. For example, signatories to the Human Rights Conventions should be required to confirm that their projects and programs are consistent with their obligations under these Conventions.

The BWIs need to publicly pledge to protect private actors who participate in BWI operations and could suffer reprisals as a result. They should make public their commitment to deny new loan requests to a state found to be retaliating against anyone who has sought to participate in the design or implementation of BWI-funded projects or programs. In extreme cases, they should suspend disbursements on existing loans.

BWI collaboration with relevant specialized agencies and regional organizations should include joint training and staff exchange programs. It should also involve ongoing dialogue on matters of mutual interest. NGOs should be able to broadly participate in these programs and discussions.

Mechanisms must be established for public participation in all aspects of BWI operations. These mechanisms should include:

- the opening of decision-making fora to public scrutiny. This could include allowing the public to attend some Board of Directors and Board of Governors meetings.

- the establishment of bodies of independent experts, with broad community participation, that have the authority to seek and receive information from BWI staff and to receive publicly disclosable explanations from the staff for their failure to follow the advice of these independent experts.[55]

- more transparent administrative procedures. One possible course would be to submit a proposed rule or procedure for public comment to which the BWIs would be required to respond.[56]

- more transparent and participatory substantive policymaking procedures. These should include an opportunity for public comment on draft policies and a requirement that the BWIs explain their responses to these comments.

Finally the BWIs should develop codes of conduct for staff that recognize their obligations both to the BWIs and to the other stakeholders in their operations.

All these measures can be achieved under the existing charters of international organizations.[57] However, the BWIs will have to reinterpret their charters using traditional means for interpreting legal texts. It should be recognized that because of the nature of the challenges facing the BWIs, these measures will not resolve them all. They will instead create the mechanisms and the atmosphere that will allow stakeholders to participate in the debate and make it possible for them to hold the BWIs accountable for their actions. Over time, these changes should make it easier to fashion an international consensus on sustainable and equitable development, and on the design of the organizations needed to promote such development.

To facilitate these measures, specialized agencies and regional arrangements also need to develop transparent and accountable governance procedures. They must produce operationally useful guidelines in their areas of expertise and must work with the BWIs to incorporate these guidelines into their policies and programs. In addition, they should deal with issues of particular interest to the BWIs in their country and thematic reports. NGOs should be invited to participate in this process.

Finally, NGOs have a crucial role to play in changing international institutional arrangements. They should educate their own governments on the need for changes in these arrangements and organize their constituents to campaign for them. Success in these efforts could create the opportunity for even more dramatic changes. Ultimately, it could make possible formal participation by non-state actors in such international organizational issues as voting, electing officials, supervising compliance and developing structures for direct participation in decision making.

CONCLUSION

The world has changed dramatically since the 1944 Bretton Woods conference. However, the institutional structures and relations that were created at that time have remained relatively static. The BWIs have responded to this disjuncture between their actual work and their institutional arrangements with *ad hoc* policy and procedural changes. The authors have argued that these responses are inadequate, are not based on sound legal principles and do not promote the rule of law. The BWIs must ensure that their actions and policies are consistent with the general principles of international law, and that they enable other international actors to conform to them. A number of steps that the BWIs can take to comply with the international legal order have been examined. These actions will also promote equitable, sustainable and participatory development.

Notes

1. See UN Charter, Article 2, para. 7; Louis Henkin, *How Nations Behave: Law and Foreign Policy* (New York: Praeger, 1968), p. 17.
2. The United Nations is able to address any issue of interest to the international community. See International Court of Justice, 'Reparation for Injuries Suffered in the Service of the United Nations, Advisory Opinion' in *International Court of Justice Reports, 1949*, p. 174.
3. In reality, based on a strict distinction between domestic and international issues, the executive branch of government assumed almost exclusive powers in international affairs. The erosion of that distinction has led to a situation in which the executive's exclusive power in international affairs has assumed a less democratic character. In particular, since the legislative branch of government most directly represents civil society, the executive's international authority has created a substantial obstacle to efforts by civil society members to participate in affairs that directly affect them. These actors have been forced to adopt a broader definition of their spheres of interest, and are beginning to think and act globally as well as locally. See papers prepared for the 'Conference on Changing Notions of Sovereignty and the Role of Private Actors in International Law', published in *The American University Journal of International Law and Policy*, vol. 9, no. 1 (1993), pp. 1–214.
4. In some cases, for example, the International Labour Organisation (which predates World War II), member states did allow non-state actors to participate in the organization's work. However, they did not allow non-state actors to join international organizations in their own right.
5. Article 2(7) of the UN Charter precludes the United Nations from intervening 'in matters which are essentially within the domestic jurisdiction' of the state or from requiring member states 'to submit such matters to settlement' under the Charter. The phrase 'domestic jurisdiction' in the Charter underscored the international community's perception that there was a set of purely domestic issues and a set of purely international issues. The United Nations would have the authority to address only the purely international issues. See Henkin, *How Nations Behave*, p. 174. The BWIs were also required to respect member states' sovereignty over their internal affairs and the World Bank was precluded from considering 'political' issues in its lending decisions.

6. Chapter VII of the UN Charter did authorize the Security Council to take coercive action of a military, economic or political nature, against a member state deemed to be a threat to international peace. In practice, however, the veto power of the permanent members of the Security Council has prevented decisive action in most cases. This was particularly relevant during the Cold War. See Alan M. James, 'Unit Veto Dominance in United Nations Peace-Keeping' in Lawrence Finkelstein (ed.), *Politics in The United Nations System* (Durham, NC: Duke University Press, 1988), p. 75.

7. UN Charter, Articles 10 and 11. The development of an International Bill of Rights, having as its point of departure the UN Charter, is a good example of the impact that the General Assembly can have on the behavior of the member states.

8. See Öztemir A. Özgür, *Apartheid: The United Nations and Peaceful Change in South Africa* (Dobbs Ferry, NY: Transnational Publishers, 1982).

9. In practice, enforcement of IMF rules depends on how a member's deviation manifested itself. Where members' monetary policies produce balance-of-payments problems that require the IMF's financial assistance, the IMF uses conditionality policies to enforce its rules. In all other cases the IMF would use consultations and peer pressure to encourage members to abide by its rules. See Joseph Gold, 'Strengthening the Soft International Law Exchange Arrangements' in Joseph Gold (ed.), *Legal and Institutional Aspects of the International Monetary System: Selected Essays*, vol. 2 (Washington, DC: International Monetary Fund, 1984), p. 515 and pp. 527–30; Richard W. Edwards, *International Monetary Collaboration* (Dobbs Ferry, NY: Transnational Publishers, 1985), pp. 638–42.

10. The World Bank classifies member countries according to their GNP per capita. Those that have a GNP per capita of less than $4,715 (in 1993 dollars) are entitled to borrow from the Bank. Citizens of all Bank member countries are eligible to bid on World Bank contracts. In 1991, the US General Accounting Office calculated that for each dollar the United States contributes to the Bank, it receives approximately $1.16 in new business. *Practices and Policies of International Financial Institutions, Hearing before the Subcommittee on International Development, Finance, Trade and Monetary Policy of the Committee on Banking, Finance and Urban Affairs*, US House of Representatives, 102nd Congress, 2nd Session, January 29, 1992, p. 57.

11. See Daniel D. Bradlow (ed.), *International Borrowing*, 3rd edition (Washington, DC: International Law Institute, 1994), which provides a sample IBRD loan agreement and a sample IDA credit agreement.

12. See Hans W. Singer, 'Rethinking Bretton Woods: From an Historical

Perspective' in Jo Marie Griesgraber and Bernhard G. Gunter (eds), *Rethinking Bretton Woods*, vol. 1, *Promoting Development: Effective Global Institutions for the Twenty-first Century*, chapter 1 (London: Pluto Press with the Center of Concern, 1995).

13. For example, see Daniel D. Bradlow, 'The International Monetary Fund, The World Bank Group and Debt Management' in *Legal Aspects of Debt Management* (Geneva: United Nations Institute of Training and Research, 1993), module V.

14. See Anthony Killick and Graham R. Bird (eds), *The IMF and Stabilization: Developing Country Experiences* (New York: St. Martin's Press, 1984); Giovanni A. Cornia, Richard Jolly and Frances Stewart (eds), *Adjustment With a Human Face – Protecting the Vulnerable and Promoting Growth*, vol. 1, A UNICEF Study (Oxford: Clarendon Press, 1987).

15. See Paul Mosley, Jane Harrigan and John Toye, *Aid and Power: The World Bank and Policy-Based Lending*, vol. 1 (London: Routledge, 1991) pp. 65–7; Ibrahim F.I. Shihata, *The World Bank in a Changing World: Selected Essays* (Boston: Dordrecht; Norwell, MA: M. Nijhoff Publishers, 1991); Joan M. Nelson (ed.), *Economic Crisis and Policy Choice: The Politics of Economic Adjustment in Developing Nations* (Princeton, NJ: Princeton University Press, 1990), Introduction, pp. 3–4. There is an intense debate over how successful these conditions have been in promoting sustainable development. Many countries that have undergone BWI-funded adjustment programs have experienced, in addition to macroeconomic stability and increased growth rates, widening income disparities, declining standards of human welfare and deteriorating environments. See Patricia Adams, 'The World Bank and the IMF in Sub-Saharan Africa: Undermining Development and Environmental Sustainability' in *Journal of International Affairs*, vol. 46, no. 1, (1992), pp. 97–117; Walden F. Bello, *Dark Victory: The United States, Structural Adjustment and Global Poverty* (London: Pluto Press with the Transnational Institute; Oakland: Food First with the Transnational Institute, 1994) pp. 32–65.

16. It should be noted that the Bank does seek to limit the issues it considers in examining a country's governance. See, for example, World Bank, *Governance and Development* (Washington, DC: World Bank, 1992). However, the distinctions it seeks to draw are arbitrary and ultimately unsustainable. Its ability to be an active participant is enhanced by its influence over the borrower country's other potential sources of funds.

17. The most significant example of this is the World Bank's adoption of a new information disclosure policy and establishment of an independent Inspection Panel in 1994. The panel investigates complaints from directly affected private parties regarding the World Bank's

failure to follow its own operating rules and procedures. See generally Daniel D. Bradlow, 'International Organizations and Private Complaints: The Case of the World Bank Inspection Panel' in *Virginia Journal of International Law*, vol. 34, no. 3 (Spring 1994) pp. 553–613.

18. See Samuel Paul and Arturo Israel (eds), *Non-governmental Organizations and the World Bank* (Washington, DC: World Bank, 1991); Ibrahim F.I. Shihata, 'The World Bank and Non-Governmental Organizations' in *Cornell International Law Journal*, vol. 25 (1992) pp. 623–41. World Bank Operational Directive 2.20 'Involving Non-governmental Organizations in Bank-Supported Activities' (Washington, DC: World Bank, October 1989), pp. 14–70. For the view that '[i]n Fund operations, NGOs do not play any role at all', see Richard Gerster, 'Accountability of Executive Directors in the Bretton Woods Institutions' in *Journal of World Trade*, vol. 27, no. 6 (1993), pp. 87–116. It should be noted that the charters of both organizations require the BWIs to deal with their member states through the Ministry of Finance, the Central Bank, or some other agency designated by the state. This requirement may act as a constraint on the BWIs' ability to interact with non-governmental actors.

19. The top 500 TNCs account for 30 per cent of the world's gross product, 70 per cent of world trade and 80 per cent of world investment. See N. Olyers, 'Gross Reality of Global Statistics' in *The Weekly Mail and Guardian*, May 13–19, 1994, p. 22.

20. See Peter H. Lewis, 'On the Internet, Dissidents' Shots Heard 'Round the World' in the *New York Times*, June 5, 1994, section E, p. 18; Howard Frederick, 'Computer Networks and the Emergence of Global Civil Society' in Linda M. Harasim (ed.), *Global Networks: Computers and International Communication* (Cambridge, MA: Massachusetts Institute of Technology Press, 1993), p. 238.

21. Martin Walker, *The Waking Giant: Gorbachev's Russia* (New York: Pantheon Books, 1986), p. 59; Wilson P. Dizard and S. Blake Swensrud, *Gorbachev's Information Revolution: Controlling Glasnost in a New Electronic Era* (Boulder, CO: Westview Press, 1987).

22. A good example is the regulation of the banking industry. Since banks now have the ability and the client-driven need to instantaneously move funds around the world, it is no longer possible for individual nations to effectively regulate their banks. In the absence of a world central bank that has global jurisdiction, the only sustainable regulatory framework is one that has the support of all participating banks and financial actors. If the framework does not have their support, they can move their money and activities to non-participating jurisdictions.

23. Universal Declaration of Human Rights, December 10, 1948, UN General Assembly, Resolution 217A (III), UN Document A/810 (1948).

24. Progress has been greater at the regional than at the global level, particularly in Europe and the Western Hemisphere. See Hurst Hannum (ed.), *Guide to International Human Rights Practice*, 2nd edition [edited for the International Human Rights Law Group] (Philadelphia: University of Pennsylvania Press, 1992); Claudio Grossman, 'Disappearances in Honduras: The Need for Direct Victim Representation in Human Rights Litigation' in *Hastings International and Comparative Law Review*, vol. 15 (1992), pp. 363–89.

25. See *Vienna Declaration* and *Program of Action*, World Conference on Human Rights, UN Document A/Conf. 15712, June 14–25, 1993. Over 1,500 NGOs represented by more than 3,000 participants from all regions of the world participated in the World Conference in Vienna, Summer 1993, influencing the conference agenda on an unprecedented level. See *The Report of the NGO Forum*, UN Document A/Conf. 15717.

26. These so-called third generation rights focus on such issues as the right to development, democracy, and a clean environment. See Philip Alston, 'A Third Generation of Solidarity Rights: Progressive Development or Obfuscation of International Human Rights Law?' in *Netherlands International Law Review*, vol. 29 (1982), pp. 307–22. See Thomas M. Frank, 'The Emerging Right to Democratic Governance' in *American Journal of International Law*, vol. 86 (January 1992), pp. 46–91; United Nations Commission on Human Rights, 'Global Consultation on the Right to Development as a Human Right', Report prepared by the Secretary General, UN Document E/CN.4/9/Rev.1. (1990); UN General Assembly, 'Declaration on Right to Development', Resolution 41/128, December 4, 1986.

27. See, for example, Katarina Tomasevski, 'Human Rights Impact Assessment: Proposals for the Next 50 Years of Bretton Woods' in Jo Marie Griesgraber and Bernhard G. Gunter (eds), *Rethinking Bretton Woods*, vol. 1, *Promoting Development: Effective Global Institutions for the Twenty-first Century*, chapter 4 (London: Pluto Press with the Center of Concern, 1995). Amartya Sen, the economist, has stated: 'There has never been a famine in any country that's been a democracy with a relatively free press. I know of no exception. It applies to very poor countries with democratic systems as well as to rich ones.' (*New York Times*, January 17, 1993, section 4, p. 1) See also Jean Drèze and Amartya Sen, *Hunger and Public Action* (Oxford: Clarendon Press; New York: Oxford University Press, 1989), pp. 263–4.

28. The BWIs have argued that they are not legally bound by the deci-

sions of the United Nations or other global or regional international organizations. See Ibrahim F.I. Shihata, 'Human Rights, Development and International Financial Institutions' in *The American University Journal of International Law and Policy*, vol. 8, no. 1 (1992), pp. 27–37; Samuel A. Bleicher, 'UN vs. IBRD' in *International Organization*, vol. 24 (1970), pp. 31–47; Statement by Aron Broches, IBRD General Counsel, to the Fourth Committee of the UN General Assembly on November 28, 1966, in *International Legal Materials*, vol. 61 (1967), pp. 150–87.

29. See Alston, 'A Third Generation of Solidarity Rights'.

30. For example, see Herman E. Daly and John B. Cobb, Jr, *For the Common Good: Redirecting the Economy towards Community, the Environment and a Sustainable Future* (Boston: Beacon Press, 1989); Robert Repetto, *Wasting Assets and Natural Resources in the National Income Accounts* (Washington, DC: World Resources Institute, 1989); Edith B. Weiss, *In Fairness to Future Generations: International Law, Common Patrimony and Intergenerational Equity* (Tokyo: United Nations University; Dobbs Ferry, NY: Transnational Publishers, 1989), pp. 45–6.

31. For example, see 'Guidelines for Incorporating Social Assessment and Participation into Bank Projects', Draft Memorandum (Washington, DC: World Bank, February 14, 1994); Bhuvan Bhatagar and Aubrey C. Williams (eds), 'Participatory Development and the World Bank: Potential Directions for Change' in *World Bank Discussion Papers*, no. 183 (Washington, DC: World Bank, 1992); *World Bank Annual Report 1994* (Washington, DC: World Bank, 1995) Participation Fund, pp. 35–6; Participation Sourcebook, pp. 46–7.

32. Richard Gerster, 'A New Framework for Accountability for the International Monetary Fund' in John Cavanagh, Daphne Wysham and Marcos Arruda (eds), *Beyond Bretton Woods: Alternatives to the Global Economic Order* (London: Pluto Press with the Institute for Policy Studies and the Transnational Institute, 1994), pp. 94–106.

33. The global effort to assist famine victims in Africa in the 1980s is a good example of this sense of solidarity and of how it can be stimulated by private actors and facilitated by the ease of global communications. See Frances Westley, 'Bob Geldof and Live Aid: The Effective Side of Global Social Innovation' in *Human Relations*, vol. 44 (1991), pp. 1011–36; Paul McGrath, 'Delivering Live Aid' in *MacLean's*, vol. 98 (1985), p. 17.

34. Under the original IMF Articles of Agreement, all member states were bound to maintain relatively fixed exchange rates. The IMF could limit its concerns to those issues which directly affected the member state's ability to maintain its currency's par value. Under the present system of free exchange rates, all factors can affect a

country's ability to maintain a stable balance-of-payments position. Thus the IMF must be concerned with all aspects of a member state's economy.

35. See note 15.
36. See Thomas Hutchins, 'Using the International Court of Justice to Check Human Rights Abuses in World Bank Projects' in *Columbia Human Rights Law Review*, vol. 23 (1991), pp. 487–524.
37. In general, it can be assumed that the BWIs should perform their functions in a way that supports the fundamental rights of individuals and peoples. Additional obligations would vary from country to country, depending on the treaties signed by individual states.
38. An interesting example is the International Labour Organisation, where employers, workers and governments participate in some policymaking activities.
39. According to Article V(6)(a) of the IBRD's Articles of Agreement, the Advisory Council shall consist of at least seven persons selected by the Board of Governors. This Council shall 'include representatives of banking, commercial, industrial, labor and agricultural interests'.
40. Article IV(10) states 'The Bank and its officers shall not interfere in the political affairs of any member; nor shall they be influenced in their decision by the political character of the member concerned. Only economic considerations shall be relevant to their decision and these considerations shall be weighed impartially to achieve the purposes stated in Article I.' Also see Article III(5)(b), stating that the purposes for which the loan is granted should be without regard to political or other 'non-economic' factors and with due regard to efficiency and economy; and Article V(5)(c), stating that the members of the Bank shall respect the international character of the duties of the staff and 'shall refrain from all attempts to influence them in the discharge of their duties'.
41. For a more detailed discussion of the Bank's interpretation of this provision, see Shihata, 'Human Rights, Development and International Financial Institutions'; and David Gillies, 'Human Rights, Democracy and Good Governance: Stretching the World Bank's Policy Frontiers' in Jo Marie Griesgraber and Bernhard G. Gunter (eds), *Rethinking Bretton Woods*, vol. 3, *The World Bank: Lending on a Global Scale*, chapter 5 (London: Pluto Press with the Center of Concern, forthcoming).
42. The more powerful member states have always recognized that the Bank's work is inherently political and, on occasion, have been willing to use the Bank to help resolve problems with states with whom they had political differences. Chile, Nicaragua and China are good examples of such cases. See Bartram S. Brown, *The United States*

and the Politicization of the World Bank: Issues of International Law and Policy* (Geneva: Graduate Institute of International Studies, 1992).

43. For a more detailed discussion of the Panel, see Bradlow, 'International Organizations and Private Complaints'.

44. See World Bank Operational Directive 2.20 (Washington, DC: World Bank, October 1989). Also see Richard E. Feinberg, 'The Changing Relationship between the World Bank and the International Monetary Fund' in *International Organization*, vol. 42 (Summer 1988), p. 545; Hiroyaki Hino, 'IMF–World Bank Collaboration' in *Finance and Development*, vol. 23 (1986), p. 10.

45. The Policy Framework Paper may be distributed to the country's other official donors, and with its consent, to non-governmental sources. See World Bank Operational Directive 2.20; Policy Framework Papers, para. 31.

46. See Article IV(2), Agreement Between the United Nations and the International Monetary Fund, 16 UNTS 328, 332 (1948); Art. IV (2) Agreement Between the United Nations and the World Bank, 16 UNTS 346, 348 (1948).

47. See Shihata, 'Human Rights, Development and International Financial Institutions'; Bleicher, 'UN vs. IBRD'; Broches, Statement of IBRD General Counsel to the Fourth Committee of the UN General Assembly.

48. See Broches, Statement of IBRD General Counsel to the Fourth Committee of the UN General Assembly. The one exception to their position is that the BWIs appear to recognize their obligation to follow binding UN Security Council resolutions, adopted pursuant to Chapter 7 of the UN Charter.

49. There is a comparable increase in the interactions between the BWIs and regional organizations which often have substantive areas of expertise similar to the international organizations.

50. See Cornia *et al.*, *Adjustment With a Human Face*. See also Richard H. Demuth, 'Relations With Other Multilateral Agencies' in John P. Lewis and Ishan Kapur (eds), *The World Bank Group, Multilateral Aid and the 1970s* (Lexington, MA: Lexington Books, 1973).

51. Other international organizations also must respond to the interconnectedness of problems and the blurring of jurisdictional boundaries. For example, environmental organizations need to incorporate the interests of workers, consumers and the unemployed into their work, and human rights organizations need to carefully assess how human rights fit into the development process and how they can work with the BWIs to promote a development process sensitive to human rights.

52. The structure of the newly established Global Environment Facility,

in which the World Bank, the United Nations Environment Programme and the United Nations Development Programme all provide the GEF's staff, may prove to be a useful model in this regard. See 'Instrument For the Establishment of the Restructured Global Environment Facility', Report of the GEF Participants Meeting, March 14–16, 1994 (March 31, 1994).

53. The Relationship Agreement does not preclude the BWIs from following United Nations decisions, but it does not require it. Security Council decisions adopted under Chapter 7 of the United Nations Charter, however, are binding on the BWIs. See Shihata, 'Human Rights, Development and International Financial Institutions', p. 32.

54. The member state could declare its willingness to provide this information in the Letter of Intent it submits to the IMF as part of its request for IMF financing.

55. This recommendation can be most easily adopted by the World Bank, which could reactivate and strengthen the IBRD's Advisory Council. The IMF and the regional development banks would need to amend their charters before implementing it.

56. At present, the BWIs often do informally seek the views of nongovernmental actors on proposed policies and programs. This practice should be formalized and rendered transparent.

57. The authors have limited their proposals to those largely achievable within the existing charters of the BWIs, because in the present political climate it is not likely that the international community would agree to amend them substantially to make the organizations more democratic. Furthermore, prudence suggests that the elasticity of these charters should be fully explored before the international community embarks on the politically risky task of seeking major charter amendments.

3. Multilateral Development Banks: Towards a New Division of Labor

Roy Culpeper

INTRODUCTION

The World Bank, the world's first multilateral development bank (MDB), was founded, along with the International Monetary Fund (IMF), at Bretton Woods in 1944. Over the following five decades, a whole family of MDBs was spawned, including, most recently, the North American Development Bank and the North Africa and Middle East Development Bank. Ironically, even though the World Bank model has proved durable and replicable, the 50th anniversary (indeed, the last decade) has occasioned trenchant criticisms of this 'grandmother' of MDBs. Indeed, a vociferous community of NGOs has mounted a highly effective campaign under the slogan of '50 Years is Enough', aimed at sweeping reforms of both the World Bank and the IMF. Some critics, including those at the *laissez-faire* end of the political spectrum, even argue that the World Bank has outlived its usefulness and should be shut down.[1]

While the author does not share the views of the 'terminators', he is sympathetic to current demands to make all the international financial institutions (IFIs) more effective, accountable and transparent agencies. The general case for reform, and Canada's role in securing change, have been addressed by the author in *Canada and the Global Governors*[2] and, with Andrew Clark, in *High Stakes, Low Incomes*.[3] The objective of this chapter is more specific, pertaining to the question: what does, or should, a reform agenda imply for relationships among the international financial institutions? In particular, what are the implications for other members of the family of MDBs, which are similar in many respects to the World Bank but have, by and large, escaped its scathing critics?[4]

THE PRINCIPAL MDBs: A COMPARISON

There is a large and growing number of MDBs, if one includes all the 'sub-regional' banks such as the Caribbean Development Bank and the Central American Bank for Economic Integration, along with a host of similar agencies in Africa and the Middle East. Excluding these, however, the core group of MDBs comprises five institutions: the World Bank, founded in 1944; the Inter-American Development Bank (IDB), founded in 1959; the African Development Bank (AfDB), founded in 1964; the Asian Development Bank (ADB), founded in 1966; and the European Bank for Reconstruction and Development (EBRD), founded in 1991. Since the EBRD is still in its infancy and has little by way of an operational record for comparison, this chapter will concentrate on the World Bank plus the other three regional development banks (RDBs).

The first point to note is that only the World Bank (along with the IMF) is formally part of the UN system as a specialized agency, although its governance has been entirely distinct and separate from the rest of the UN family. The Bretton Woods twins were established as the economic part of the post-war international order, parallel to the political organs of the United Nations. But while the UN organs adhere to the principle of 'one country, one vote', the two Bretton Woods institutions were established on the model of corporate governance, with a weighted voting system favoring larger shareholders, that is, roughly 'one dollar, one vote'. This gives the developed countries (OECD), which are in a minority in the United Nations and home to only about 15 per cent of humanity, a distinct majority in the Bretton Woods institutions (BWIs). The power and influence of the developed countries over the BWIs has profoundly affected more than the behavior of these agencies. Developed countries tend to view the BWIs as more effective, and are accordingly more inclined to give priority in allocating their financial and other resources to these agencies, rather than those of the United Nations.

In contrast, the RDBs have no formal linkage to the United Nations – they are not even recognized as specialized agencies. The absence of such linkages is due to the historical circumstances leading to their establishment and, in particular, to the geopolitical setting of the Cold War. In other words, they were envisaged not as agencies of a universal order, but as institutions with an implicit role in regional development. Membership in the RDBs comprised the regional borrowing members, on the one hand, and regional plus non-regional non-borrowing members, on the other. The latter category in all cases was dominated by the Western alliance (including Japan). It is no accident that, after decades of resistance by the United States, the IDB was established on the eve of the Cuban revolution, or that the Asian Development Bank was established during the Vietnam War, again after years of indifference by the United States.[5]

This is not to say that the RDBs were ever 'pawns' of the Western alliance. Indeed, the economic and political aspirations of developing countries in the respective regions were at least as important as the geostrategic interests of the alliance. In all three regions, developing countries felt they could get a better deal by cooperating with each other rather than by being dependent on the Washington-based BWIs, in which they had little voice. Moreover, because they were in a double minority in those organizations (a minority among developing countries, which in turn were in a minority overall), control by regional members became a fundamental cornerstone of the RDB charters.[6]

Some three decades after the establishment of the RDBs, the World Bank still overshadows the regional banks in size, scope and influence. The subscribed capital of the World Bank in 1993 was 70 per cent greater than the combined capital of the other three, and its full-time staff was 60 per cent greater.

Table 3.1
The World Bank and the RDBs: Indicators of Relative Size, 1993

	World Bank	IDB	AfDB	ADB
Capital (US $B)	170.0	54.2	21.0	23.1
Disbursements (US $B)	16.1	3.7	2.2	2.9
Staff	6,388	1,818	1,244	1,898
Number of loans	288	74	133	78

Source: Annual Reports

Recently, however (particularly since about the mid-1980s), the RDBs have grown rapidly, due to large capital increases negotiated by the members. As a result, the lending capacity of each of the RDBs in its respective region began to close the gap with that of the World Bank in the same region. Indeed, the IDB's lending capacity equalled that of the World Bank in Latin America and the Caribbean by 1992 and is poised to overtake it in the wake of a large capital increase concluded in 1994. The Asian Development Bank also completed negotiations for a large capital increase in 1994 and may be expected to rival the World Bank as a lender to Asian countries in future years. Only the African Development Bank is likely to continue to lag behind the World Bank in lending to its region for some time.

Thus, the MDBs (with one exception) are experiencing similar growth in terms of their relative size as lenders to developing regions.[7] They are also similar in other ways, including the distribution of their loans among various sectors, and the kinds of projects and programs they support.[8] The World Bank and the regional bank frequently cooperate in delivering the same project, as co-financiers in a larger consortium. Finally, they all compete for the same pools of capital – whether from the national or international bond markets for their non-concessional lending, or from official development assistance (ODA) budgets for their concessional lending.

At the same time, there remain important differences – and therefore some complementarity – between the World Bank and the MDBs. In 1977, the World Bank initiated 'structural adjustment' lending, which is geared to bringing about macro- and microeconomic policy changes in recipient countries. It took most of the decade for all the RDBs to emulate the World Bank by initiating their own policy-based lending programs. But even today in policy-based lending there is considerable differentiation between the World Bank's activities and those of the regional banks. To begin with, the adjustment programs are typically designed by the World Bank, often in association with the IMF in Washington. To the extent the RDB participates, it is as a co-financier, with little or no input on policy design or implementation. And the Asian Bank has limited its policy-based lending program to *sectoral* adjustment operations, that is, it has chosen not to get involved in macroeconomic policy-based lending.

The World Bank has (along with the IMF) established its pre-eminence in policy-based lending principally because of its substantial research activities, which far outstrip those of the RDBs. Nor is this true only of adjustment issues. Its annual flagship publication, *World Development Report*, has analyzed issues concerning infrastructure (as in 1994), the health sector (1993) and the environment (1992). Similarly, its quarterly *Finance and*

Development, published in association with the IMF, has a reputation as a forum for 'leading edge' debates on development policy. In addition, there is a veritable torrent of publications, ranging from narrowly-focused research papers to bulky tomes on the political economy of poverty.

Although each of the RDBs has an active program of research, it is not unfair to say that none commands the authority of the World Bank. Moreover, the major development issues of the day, even if they have a specific regional focus, tend to be researched by the World Bank rather than the corresponding RDB.[9] Thus, it is clear that the policy agenda on development is shaped to a far greater extent by the World Bank than by the regional banks, individually or collectively.

A NEW DIVISION OF LABOR AMONG MDBs

New Challenges and Expectations

Is the current division of labor among the MDBs satisfactory? Should there be even more complementarity than there is now? Before considering these questions, it is appropriate to consider new challenges and expectations which have arisen for all the multilateral banks.

Since the 1980s, there have been debates over the rationale of structural adjustment lending, as well as deepening concerns about the environmental impact of development projects and the sustainability of long-run economic growth, plus greater sensitivity to the gender dimension of development. These all led to new demands being placed on the activities and performance of the MDBs (along with those of the bilateral development agencies). For example, not only is environmental impact assessment now a key aspect of project design; good stewardship of the environment has also become the basis of new MDB activities, as with the Global Environment Facility (GEF), jointly administered by the World Bank, the United Nations Development Programme (UNDP) and United Nations Environment Programme (UNEP).

The gender dimension has also appeared in the MDBs' agenda, although with less to show for it. The need to ensure that women and girls are equal beneficiaries of MDB interventions is now widely acknowledged, although resistance both among borrowing countries and within the MDBs themselves has made the operationalization of the gender dimension problematic.

More hopefully, the debate on the distributional impact of structural adjustment has led to the reaffirmation of poverty alleviation as the *raison d'être* of all the MDBs. Similarly, the debate has led to an emphasis on human resource development, with a substantial shift in lending patterns toward the social sectors – health, education, population and nutrition – and a reduction in the relative share of large-scale infrastructure projects in the energy and transportation sectors. Finally, issues of governance are now raised with borrowing countries, including questions which were hardly ever entertained during the Cold War, such as corruption and the accountability and transparency of governments.

Such issues comprise much of the agenda for the reform of the MDBs in the 1990s. These new imperatives, while urgent and overdue, have also greatly increased the complexity of the MDBs' operations. Their erstwhile mission, to facilitate economic growth via projects with a high rate of economic return, was difficult enough to achieve. But now 'development' is seen to encompass multi-dimensional objectives, embracing social, cultural and even political domains.[10]

To complicate matters still further, all four MDBs have recently commissioned reviews of the state of their lending portfolios; the World Bank began such a review in 1992 and the others followed. These reviews have emerged with astonishingly similar conclusions. In particular, they all emphasized the urgent need to move away from a 'volume' or 'approval culture' – that is, a system biased toward an ever-growing quantity of loans[11] – and toward better *quality* lending. In the case of the World Bank, a doubling in the percentage of unsuccessful projects during the 1980s illustrated the underlying deterioration in portfolio quality. None of the RDBs was willing (or even able) to quantify the extent of portfolio deterioration in the same way as the World Bank, but their analysis points in similar directions.

Moreover, all the MDBs have drawn similar policy implications from these reviews. A shift from quantity to quality lending will mean better design, implementation and supervision of projects and programs. It will also require demonstrating 'development results' or outcomes of MDB activity, viewed at the country level. All the MDBs have accordingly embraced country assistance strategies to define better-quality lending programs as well as to evaluate the results of those programs. Under such strategies, a unitary framework is being put in place, within which each country's objective circumstances, its development plans and aspirations, its policies, the assistance programs and projects of various external agencies, and the development outcomes (growth, poverty levels, investment, social indicators) over time can be assessed in a holistic manner.

Key Principles of a New Division of Labor

These new challenges and expectations greatly raise the stakes in the MDBs' reform agenda. More is demanded of them than ever, both in terms of inputs (better designed and implemented operations) and outputs (more tangible results in the borrowing countries). Demands for reform have also come at a time of fiscal constraint in most non-borrowing (donor) countries, which provide the lion's share of MDB resources. The recently-concluded eighth replenishment of the IDB, designed to sustain a level of lending of $7 billion indefinitely, was purportedly its last. The era of rapid expansion among the MDBs, which characterized the 1970s and 1980s, may be over. Donor countries are, in effect, telling the MDBs to do more with less, or, at any rate, to produce better development outcomes within the same constrained resource envelope.

Such messages may on the surface appear negative, but they also serve to reaffirm the purpose of the MDBs. After all, concerns about poverty eradication, environmental impact, the gender dimension and good governance are 'externalities' not readily accommodated by market forces alone. Indeed, these concerns are still by and large external to the MDBs themselves, given their adoption of the corporate paradigm (with an objective of economic rate of return, rather than pure profit). It will take continuing vigilance by the membership to ensure that the MDBs implement the new agenda facing them. But as long as the world community attaches importance to the larger dimensions of development, the MDBs are likely to be more, not less, important as 'agencies of global governance'.

Seen in this context, the question of *what* the MDBs do is likely to dominate questions of *how* they accomplish their objectives, including the question of 'new relationships' among them set out at the beginning of this paper. The fact is that all MDBs are expected to achieve much more ambitious development targets than they have ever attempted heretofore.

This means considerable capacity-building, particularly in the RDBs, as the requisite staff are hired for or reallocated to new programs. The process of capacity-building will be most demanding at the African Development Bank, which is in the midst of a political crisis.[12] The other two RDBs, which have just received a vote of confidence from their memberships in the form of substantial capital replenishments, are in a much better position to 're-tool'.

There is, none the less, a temptation, prompted by fiscal constraint, for larger (industrial country) shareholders, to say: 'Let the World Bank be reaffirmed in its lead role among the MDBs – it is the most experienced and best-positioned to meet the new challenges. The regional banks should continue in a subsidiary role, at most.' Such an argument would incline toward a strengthening of existing complementarities and a reduction of overlaps. The World Bank would continue to dominate in policy-setting and in research on the most important development issues.

A reaffirmation of the status quo among MDBs might be perceived by industrial countries in their best interest, but would not necessarily serve either the MDBs or the developing countries well. A fundamental lesson learned from post-war experience is that successful, sustainable development does not result exclusively from the assistance provided by outside agencies. Instead, the success stories have usually resulted from the initiatives of the developing countries themselves, with external agents playing a catalytic role. Another lesson of post-war experience is that there is not necessarily one path to success. The development strategies pursued by Japan, Korea and Taiwan involved considerably more state intervention or market guidance than is considered appropriate today by the BWIs.[13]

The above considerations suggest that certain interrelated principles might inform relationships between and among developing countries and external agents such as the MDBs. These are:

- competitive pluralism, which refers to the need for different approaches to development. It suggests that a certain amount of overlap between organizations is inevitable, and that too much complementarity may be undesirable. This may lead on occasion to differences between the organizations as to appropriate policy prescriptions for particular countries. Rather than being shunned as disruptive, such differences could yield substantial benefits, in particular, the generation of alternative ideas and experiences from which lessons could be learned and 'best practice' approaches could emerge.

- devolution, which refers to the shedding of power and responsibility for planning and implementing development projects, from 'higher' to 'lower' authorities – that is, from the Bretton Woods institutions, the UN organizations and the major donor agencies to the regional and sub-regional banks and national agencies. The need for devolution goes well beyond the MDB group to the developing countries and their people.

Its rationale is that beneficiary participation in development projects and programs dramatically enhances their chances of success. It also helps to build capacity and human resources.

• subsidiarity, which applies to situations in which jurisdiction may be shared between two or more levels of authority. This principle suggests that lower, rather than higher, levels should be given the lead role if there is a choice or a conflict.

• increasing local ownership, which is implicit in the other three, implies that development activities and institutions which 'belong' to participants and beneficiaries are more likely to be viable and sustainable over the long run.

The next section analyzes what these four principles imply for the relationships between the RDBs and the World Bank.

FROM PRINCIPLES TO PRACTICE

Relative Size

First and foremost, the principles listed above imply that the World Bank's domination must end. It may not be possible or even desirable to close the huge gap in their relative sizes, via sufficiently large capital increases to match individual RDBs' lending capacity and staff complements with those of the World Bank. Perhaps a more reasonable target might be to achieve the kind of parity with the World Bank attained by the IDB in the Latin America/Caribbean region – both agencies having approximately the same lending capacity in the region.[14] Such a target would mean that further substantial capital increases would be required at the African and Asian Development Banks. Once approximate parity is reached, the World Bank would be constrained to maintain a lending level to the region no greater than that of the regional bank, except by mutual agreement. The target of regional parity in lending capacity is important, since the capacity to lend is the capacity to influence. The RDBs cannot hope to be contenders with the World Bank in their own regions unless they have commensurate lending capacity. The result of such adjustments would effectively create an MDB system with double the capacity of the World Bank: half would be in the World Bank itself, and the other half in the RDBs collectively. Moreover, with the shift from quantity to quality lending, and the advent of a 'sustainable' lending-level policy at the IDB, the growth rate of MDB lending may be expected to level off. Increased lending capacity can then be concentrated in the region which needs external resources most: Sub-Saharan Africa.

Institutional Capacity

Reducing the size differential alone would be insufficient, given the shift from quantity to quality lending. The RDBs need to be more equally matched with the World Bank in other respects as well. For example, the pre-eminent role of the World Bank in policy-based lending and development research needs to be balanced by more substantive roles for the RDBs in both areas. This will require investment in staff resources at the regional banks, particularly at the African Development Bank. Additional staff are needed particularly in economic and sector work (to help design economic policy reform programs).

Lead Roles in Country Assistance Strategies

As all MDBs move towards programming based on country assistance strategies, there will be a growing need to ensure the consistency of such strategies and clarify lead responsibilities. Moreover, the preparation of such strategies will provide opportunities both to avoid overlap and to promote 'competitive pluralism'. Essentially, country strategies will need a certain amount of collaboration, the sharing of data and scope for exchanges between staff members to ensure agreement as to the description and analysis of development problems, and as to the key policy prescriptions for each country. Thus, it would make sense for lead responsibility to be assigned to either the World Bank or the regional bank in the preparation of country assistance strategies. As to the choice of countries for each bank, an 'ideal' allocation might involve reserving the largest and most complex countries in each region for the World Bank, while the remainder would be the responsibility of the regional bank.[15] For example, the World Bank could be given lead responsibility in the four countries with the largest GNP in each region.

The lead role would mean principal responsibility for preparing country economic memoranda, the country assistance strategy, and the 'policy dialogue' with the country generally. It would also imply an important role in coordinating the assistance of other bilateral and multilateral agencies. Within each country assistance strategy, differing roles could be taken on by the MDBs, according to their relative strengths, knowledge of local conditions, sectoral expertise, etc. Not having a lead role would not necessarily relegate the MDB to the status of a minor lender. Moreover, it would be incumbent on the lead institution to involve others in the preparation and negotiation of the basic country strategy, and (to the extent possible) to ensure overall coherence and consistency.

Table 3.2
Proposed World Bank Lead Responsibilities in the Twelve Largest Borrowers (ranked by GNP, 1992)

Asia	Africa	Latin America
China	Algeria	Brazil
Korea[16]	Egypt	Mexico
India	Nigeria	Argentina
Indonesia	Morocco	Venezuela

Source: author

Reform of Consultative Groups

The 'lead role' would manifest itself in consultative groups and aid consortia, which bring together a recipient country with its donor community, to discuss the country's development strategy and the plans of individual donors. These meetings are typically chaired by the World Bank;[17] with devolution, the regional banks should assume this role, perhaps as co-chair with the recipient country itself, except in the largest countries. While these fora have potential for enhancing coordination among donors, in fact they tend to serve largely as 'information exchanges' for the benefit of individual donors and as pressure points in the 'policy dialogue' with recipients.

There is also scope for making such fora more transparent and open to public input, particularly from the recipient country. This would mean that presentations, in the form of written briefs or oral remarks, would be welcomed from individuals and groups other than the incumbent government and its officials. The purpose of such openness would be both to provide a channel for participation in the development planning process, as well as popular feedback on current policies and projects.

70

CONCLUSIONS: THE PROCESS OF REFORM

A new division of labor among the MDBs, such as that suggested here, would neither be easy to achieve nor implemented overnight. The new relationships should be embedded in a wider program of reform at the IFIs, designed to make the institutions more transparent and accountable as well as able to deliver results in the new multidimensional development agenda. Moreover, some resistance to change may be expected from the MDBs and their staffs – particularly at the World Bank, the influence of which would be reduced by operationalizing the principles of devolution and subsidiarity. A transitional period of a few years may be expected, during which responsibilities and perhaps even staff members may be transferred from the World Bank to the RDBs.[18]

In particular, the current political impasse at the African Development Bank needs to be resolved before that institution regains the confidence of its membership sufficiently in order to take on the much more substantive role suggested here. Among other things, a greater weight for non-regional members – less than 50 per cent of voting power to maintain African control, but more than the current statutory one-third – might be required. At the Asian Development Bank it may be time to contemplate the balance of power moving in the opposite direction, to bring about majority control for the developing member countries. Such a change could, for example, be accommodated by special capital increases to give greater shares and voting power to China and India, which may expect to have a growing voice in the affairs of their region.

Given its political nature, the entire enterprise of IFI reform needs to be deliberated and overseen by an essentially political body, which would be responsible for its design and accountable for its implementation. One possibility would be a committee of ministers like the Committee of Twenty created in 1972 to consider reforms to the international financial system.[19] Such a body would be created for a period of five years or more, during which it would meet to consider and approve reforms and oversee their initial implementation. Once the committee is satisfied that the new system is substantially in working order, it could wind itself up and allow oversight to be exercised by the formal governing bodies.

In sum, increased collaboration among the MDBs is possible and even desirable assuming no loss of identity of the relatively smaller regional development banks. The principles of devolution

71

and subsidiarity can promote greater diversity in projects and economic analysis, avoiding artificial uniformity among borrowing governments' policies. The various RDBs are likely to evolve differently: possibly more voice would be given to *non*-borrowers in the AfDB, but, in the ADB, more voice to the larger borrowers. All the banks will benefit from improved political oversight and application of principles of transparency and accountability. Collaboration among the MDBs does not need to nor should it result in merging of identities and missions.

Notes

1. See Terence Corcoran, 'It's Time to Shut the World Bank Down', *Globe and Mail*, October 4, 1994.
2. Roy Culpeper, *Canada and the Global Governors* (Ottawa: The North–South Institute, 1994).
3. Roy Culpeper and Andrew Clark, *High Stakes, Low Incomes* (Ottawa: The North–South Institute, 1994).
4. This essay does not examine the equally important but far more complex issue of the relationships between the MDBs and the United Nations family.
5. The case of the African Development Bank is different. For 18 years after its creation, membership was restricted to the African continent only. But even during this period, one could argue that the African Bank, with neither Western nor Soviet sponsorship, was in part an expression of aspirations toward 'non-alignment'. Ultimately, after membership was opened to non-regional members in 1982, this Bank followed the pattern of the other RDBs, with members of the Western alliance taking a prominent role (and with the Soviet bloc conspicuously absent).
6. For a fuller discussion of the history and political dynamics of the RDBs, see Roy Culpeper, 'Regional Development Banks: Exploiting their Specificity', in *Third World Quarterly*, vol. 15, no. 3, 1994, pp. 459–82. While *regional members* command a voting majority in all three RDBs, this has meant a majority for *developing* members only at the IDB, where Latin American members have always jealously guarded their majority stake in the face of a huge US shareholding, and at the African Bank, where a condition of opening capital to non-regional members in 1982 was a two-thirds majority for African members. At the Asian Bank, Japan, Australia and New Zealand are part of the overall regional majority, but absent these three members, developing countries have always accounted for a minority of the shareholdings.
7. Although the disbursements of the MDBs are large in annual terms,

they have always been among many sources of external capital to developing regions. Indeed, at the height of the debt crisis in 1984, when private lenders and investors shunned the Third World, MDBs provided only about 20 per cent of net resource flows to developing countries. Private flows rebounded after 1989; by 1992, the share of MDB disbursements had fallen to less than 15 per cent of total flows.

8. See Culpeper, 'Regional Development Banks: Exploiting their Specificity'.

9. Two recent examples are: World Bank, *The East Asian Miracle* (New York: Oxford University Press, 1993); and World Bank, *Adjustment in Africa* (New York: Oxford University Press, 1994).

10. All the MDBs have statutory impediments to employing 'political criteria' in carrying out their work. The prominent exception is the newly-created European Bank for Reconstruction and Development (EBRD) which has an explicit political mandate to facilitate the transition from centrally-planned to democratic, market-oriented societies. But even in the case of the other MDBs, political considerations have occasionally been employed, albeit not explicitly (an example is the cessation of lending by the MDBs to Chile under Allende). The advent of 'governance' as an issue has required the MDBs to present the issue as one of 'an enabling environment for better economic performance'. It has also meant that more explicitly political issues such as human rights and democratization are still off-limits as far as the MDBs (but not some of their critics) are concerned.

11. The most explicit manifestation was the annual lending target, which often led to a 'mad scramble' to secure approvals from the Executive Board toward the end of the fiscal year. A more subtle manifestation was the reward system for project officers, who could expect more rapid promotion for loan approvals, while the ultimate success or failure of the project figured much less as an indication of staff merit.

12. The May 1994 Annual Meetings held in Nairobi broke up in disarray, amid disputes among member countries about the Bank's policy of lending non-concessional resources to non-creditworthy countries, the resignation of senior financial managers and allegations of mismanagement.

13. Differing perceptions on the universal applicability of the 'Washington consensus' led Japan to launch a debate in the World Bank Executive Board in 1992. This sparked the World Bank's 1993 study, *The East Asian Miracle*, which did not put the debate to rest. For a critical review, see: Alice Amsden, 'Why isn't the Whole World Experimenting with the East Asian Model to Develop? Review of

The East Asian Miracle', in *World Development*, vol. 22, no. 4, April 1994, pp. 627–34.

14. This assumes that the World Bank will maintain its current allocation among regions. The current pattern is not fixed by policy.
15. The reason is that the larger countries require more resources. Moreover, larger borrowers are often less inclined to comply with the conditionality of the regional bank; on the other hand, they are apt to take the conditionality of the World Bank more seriously.
16. Editor's note: Korea graduated from World Bank lending after this chapter was written: 'Korea Graduates', *World Bank News*, vol. XIV, no. 9, March 2, 1995, pp. 1–2.
17. Except in the case of 'Roundtables' for a small number of countries, which are chaired by the UNDP.
18. Curiously, there is very little in the way of staff secondments among the MDBs. For example, the Asian Development Bank has a staff exchange program with the IMF, but none with the World Bank.
19. This idea was advanced by Gerald K. Helleiner in 1994: 'Democracy and Global Governance: Revisiting – and Revising – the Committee of 20', North–South Institute, Speech series, North–South Institute, Ottawa, Canada. Editor's note: see also *Rethinking Bretton Woods: Conference Report and Recommendations* (Washington, DC: Center of Concern, 1994) p. 9.

4. The Bretton Woods Challengers

Lisa Jordan

INTRODUCTION

In 1994, debates about globalization and the future of the international economic order centered around the Bretton Woods institutions (BWIs). But as the BWIs celebrated their 50th anniversary, not everyone joined in the applause. Many academics and activists believe that the BWIs have failed to fulfill their original mandates to absorb shocks to the global financial system and to control the global economic order in a way that would make prosperity available to all people.

The critics are looking for viable alternatives. Some look for alternative institutions to carry out the original mandates of the BWIs, though these mandates would need to be strengthened to contend with today's global financial market. Others are looking for alternatives to the particular kind of globalization and development embodied in the current practices of the BWIs.

This chapter provides a framework for examining the different types of arguments that relate to the BWIs. It begins by discussing the ideas of Walter Russel Mead and the UN Development Program (UNDP)[1] whose work sparked debate within the Rethinking Bretton Woods project. It then provides an overview of several schools of thought engaged in the Bretton Woods debate.

The critics of the BWIs tend to fall into two opposing camps, each with two subgroups. The first camp – referred to hereafter as the alternative normative challengers – is primarily comprised of alternative economists, abolitionists and activists who provide an alternative normative challenge to the BWIs. The second group of challengers, which will be called the structuralist camp, consists of structuralists and reform economists. The two groups of challengers do not necessarily contest the failures on which the other concentrates. The failure of the BWIs to regulate global capital, for example, is well understood. Moreover, there is broad agreement that:

- the more powerful countries have benefited from the BWIs;

- development as practiced by the World Bank has failed;

- the debt crisis has only been solved for a handful of powerful Western banks;

- the preclusion of debt forgiveness from consideration by the BWIs is an enormous mistake, and

- the global economy has been adjusted at the expense of the world's poor.

The goals of both groups of critics are virtually identical in general – to reform the global economy and maximize the goal of equitable, sustainable and participatory development. The present and future role of the BWIs in realizing this goal is the field of debate between the two approaches. Underlying their differences is a struggle over the significance of 'globalization'.

TWO CAMPS OF CHALLENGERS

The Alternative Normative Challenge

The alternative normative challenge emphasizes such values as self-reliance, human rights and ecological appropriateness. The main players are alternative economists, abolitionists and activists. The principal problems with the BWIs are not defined by standard economic terminology but in political and cultural language. The components of the alternative normative challenge are all-encompassing and practice-oriented but do not provide a unified, holistic alternative paradigm. Instead, this challenge serves as the basis for a series of alternatives to the 'modernization' approach to development.

Abolitionists and alternative economists believe the BWIs are already too powerful and are therefore part of the problem of disparity, not part of the solution. In general, these activists and scholars are keen on shrinking the mandate for global institutions. These arguments are most succinctly put forth by authors such as Manfred Max-Neef[2] and George Aditjondro,[3] by activists like Vandana Shiva[4] and by others in the US-based '50 Years is Enough' campaign.[5]

The most distinctive feature of the alternative normative challenge is the priority it puts on the needs of the 'local space', that is, the local community of people and the environment.[6] Development, in this school, is a process that begins in the local space, understood to be the primary space to solve the social ills faced by local populations. The debate pits the macro process of globalization against the micro space of local communities. These critics are opposed to the process of globalization that is supported by the BWIs and the modernization model of development. They believe that globalization, as embodied in the BWIs, threatens diversity, local political capacity, and key democratic concepts like representation and legitimacy. Further, they argue that this globalization unfairly benefits the already powerful. To these critics, the BWIs are, at best, Orwellian.

The Structural Challenge

In contrast, a second camp, comprised mostly of structuralists and reformist economists, believe the BWIs need more authority in order to control the flow of private global capital and other global financial processes that threaten the stability of national economies.

Those presenting this challenge tend to subscribe to the tenets of Keynesian economics. They believe that the flow, distribution, form and rate of capital exchange is at the heart of all global economic problems. In particular, they identify a shortage of capital as the principal cause of the development crisis. If the flow of global capital could be properly controlled or regulated, those social ills created by the absence of capital would be cured. Poverty, measurable by income level, can also be solved by adjustments in the capital flow. Development, for these critics, is more a goal than a process; it will flow from a healthy functioning global economy.

Further, by this argument, the global economy is stymied because narrow national interests impede a just flow of capital. The answer, then, is to raise the power of supranational economic institutions above that of nation states, thereby creating a system that is truly global in scope and free to govern with the best interests of the globe in mind. The structuralist camp wants the BWIs to adopt a broader, more powerful mandate than that which currently exists. It advocates institutions strong enough to impose a rule-based system of global economics, as opposed to the power-based system by which the world economy currently functions.

The structuralist camp took center stage in preliminary debate by participants in the Rethinking Bretton Woods project. With a predominant concern for the effects of debt in developing countries, a standard economic approach to the definition of problems associated with Bretton Woods was adopted. Walter Russell Mead's 'American Economic Policy in the Antemillennial Era'[7] was representative of reformist economists, while the United Nations Development Programme's (UNDP) *Human Development Report 1992*[8] was representative of structuralists. The debate started from the premise that the BWIs failed in the fundamental mandate to govern the movement of global capital. According to Mead: 'The Bretton Woods Institutions have failed to establish a system that would bring about economic expansion, stable prices and exchange rates and a liberal regime in international trade.'[9]

The UNDP's Human Development Report states it still more clearly:

> The IMF and the World Bank have drifted away from their original mandates ... The GATT mandate is fairly limited at present ... The IMF has failed in its role as an economic manager over the past 45 years ... In practice, there are no development institutions managing the new integrated global economy.[10]

To these challengers, the BWIs have proven incapable of placing the global public good over the interests of private financial capital, most notably in the 1980s, when free-market ideology prevailed over Keynesian economics. Both Mead and the UNDP propose a series of truly global institutions which would have the power and freedom to fulfill the original Keynesian vision for supranational controls over global finance.

TWO PRESCRIPTIONS

The Structural Prescriptions

Sustainable, participatory and equitable development is a tall order. Mead and the UNDP present similar prescriptions to reach this goal. They each respect the Keynesian vision and see it as a design to privilege the public good over private interests. The Keynesian vision can be seen as the economists' equivalent of a moral ethic that overcomes individualism and the havoc it wreaks in the global economic order. It is a response to Reaganomics gone global. For the structuralists, the solution to today's economic debacles is therefore to reaffirm Keynesian principles, either by strengthening the present BWIs or by establishing new, stronger institutions that can overcome the limitations inherent in the pursuit by industrialized nations of their own, narrower interests.

The first structural prescription for achieving equitable, sustainable and participatory development is to create an understanding of the 'megaeconomic' reality which exists in today's global financial market. Mead's proposal is the most eloquent. He calls for 'a multilateral global Keynesianism' which would

> introduce an additional megaeconomic level of intervention in the service of the Keynesian vision. The relation of megaeconomics, the economics of the international system, to macroeconomics, the economics of the nation-state is analogous to the relation of macroeconomics to the microeconomics of the firm.[11]

Once the need for a megaeconomic reality is recognized, a global central bank is necessary to begin restoring global public good over national or private interests. The purposes of the proposed bank are multiple. First, it is meant to overcome a number of weaknesses in the current global financial system, including:

- a reliance on *ad hoc* forms of international cooperation, which may not happen in time to resolve monetary crises;

- the failure of the G–7 countries to regulate their own economies in ways that would promote the megaeconomic public good, and

- the failure of the IMF to apply controls on surplus countries.

The global central bank would be in a position to:

- create a common currency;

- expand credit and stabilize prices;

- undertake expansionary policies or restrictive fiscal and monetary policy in the supranational economy;

- stabilize international currency markets, and

- provide liquidity and credits needed by poor nations.

It would be able to operate both nationally and globally:

> Globally, the International Bank would be able to affect interest rates and credit creation as any central bank does within a national economy. It would also be in a position to accommodate the special needs of individual nations and have more instruments at its disposal than the IMF did in the 1950s and 1960s.[12]

The second prescription which structuralists generally agree upon is the creation of an international trade organization. In the view of the UNDP, '[a]n international trade organization would ensure free and equal access to all forms of global trade, to manage commodity stabilization schemes and make recommendations for commodity policies.'[13]

Mead suggests it must be based on two clear premises: that goods and services produced in accordance with international standards should enjoy a type of most-favored nation status; and, goods not produced in compliance with such standards should be penalized.

Mead also emphasizes the need to return to a demand-based global trade policy, which would establish local markets, boost demand, cut back on subsidized supply programs (especially in agriculture) and reduce the suicidal level of competition now evident in the global marketplace.

These new institutions would allow the world to address the 'great contemporary economic questions' of our time. According to Mead, these questions are: how to integrate the Third World economies and the former centrally planned economies into the 'global' economy of the developed countries, and how to address the relationship between the global economy and the global environment. While the alternative normative challengers share Mead's questions, they take great exception to the framework in which he places his questions and his answers.

The Alternative Normative Prescriptions

Abolitionists and alternative economists would first take exception to the supremacy of Northern economies in the framing of both the relationship between regional economies and the relationship between economy and environment. Structuralists and Keynesian economists, Mead in this instance, tend to assume that the global economy is more important than its parts, especially its weaker parts. They perceive the global capital model to be universally respected and desired. Fundamental critiques of this model that have emerged from the 'weaker' quarters of the system are generally ignored. Categorized as 'alternative structural analyses', these marginalized critiques include the dependency thesis, the center–periphery analysis, and various structural analyses on poverty done by Asian and African scholars.[14]

Second, structuralists and Keynesians consider the environment to be definable as a 'good' or 'service', and therefore measurable in conventional economic terms. This subsumes complex integrated ecosystems into economic parts which can then be dealt with separately. Advocates of the alternative normative school would argue that the environment is a linkage issue, an issue-web, which cannot be separated from lifestyles, culture, politics or human rights. Using economics to define the environment necessarily changes the nature of the debate. Ecologists would even argue that the primary 'service' offered by the environment, that of life support, is only functional if addressed in its totality. Economics is a wholly inadequate discipline for encompassing the reality of the environment.

The alternative normative challengers vary in their criticisms of the BWIs, but they rarely define their critiques in relation to economics as it is conventionally understood. They are far more likely to define problems in terminology reflecting concepts of power and culture.

Max-Neef, an alternative economist, attempts to redefine human needs and poverty, which in turn redefines economics and development: 'The way in which needs are understood and the role and attributes ascribed to the possible satisfiers of those needs are absolutely definitive in determining a development strategy.'[15]

Max-Neef rejects the priority of needs that are satisfied by the production of economic goods. He describes the supremacy of goods production as a cultural choice, and a tool which has been chosen by Western cultures to satisfy their needs:

> In industrial capitalism, the production of economic goods along with the system of allocating them has conditioned the type of satisfiers that predominate ... The question of quality of life is overshadowed by our obsession to increase productivity.[16]

This line of thought implies rejecting the hierarchical, linear approach to satisfying human needs in favor of the understanding that needs are intertwined – a system. Development becomes the process of a person or community defining needs and choosing

81

appropriate ways to satisfy these needs. From this perspective, the BWIs and the form of development they espouse pre-empt development that begins in civil society or local space because the linear approach – embedded in those institutions – pre-empts a systemic approach to addressing human needs. Again, Max-Neef comments: 'There is no possibility for the active participation of people in gigantic systems which are hierarchically organized and where decisions flow from the top down to the bottom.'[17]

Participatory, sustainable and equitable development will not be achieved by further processes of globalization or strengthening international institutions. Max-Neef's solution lies in a new political order based on a democratic culture. He advocates developing processes of economic and political decentralization, strengthening genuine democratic institutions, and encouraging greater autonomy in the emerging social movements.[18]

Following Max-Neef's theory that development in the local space is pre-empted by globalization, George Aditjondro calls globalization an 'emerging colonialism.' Using Indonesia as an example, Aditjondro writes:

> Due to the increasing dependence on foreign aid and trade, the Indonesian government seemed to be more responsive to the up-and-downs in the World Bank and the parliaments of the donor countries, than to the aspirations of the Indonesian people, expressed through parliamentary and extra-parliamentary channels.[19]

This increasing dependency or interaction with foreign institutions creates a parallel dependency among burgeoning civil society in developing countries:

> This neo-colonial mentality has induced Indonesian dissidents from time to time to address their overt and covert lobbying campaigns to overseas targets. Besides, Southern NGOs in general have become more and more dependent on information and lobbying efforts implemented by Northern NGOs, since these organizations have better access to information concerning ongoing and upcoming projects which will be funded by the World Bank, etc. Third World NGOs have also had to suit and adapt their agendas, or sometimes completely adopt the agendas of Northern NGOs, in the preparation of international advocacy campaigns.[20]

When democracy is considered a condition for aid or trade by the same international institutions that are slowly suffocating the local political space, the dilemma becomes even more complex. The more a state responds to global institutions, the less it tends to respond to an active local constituency. This is especially true when local constituencies can only offer state legitimacy, a commodity not often necessary in today's world, while the global institution can offer a credit line, which is absolutely necessary for state survival.

While Max-Neef focuses on the theoretical underpinnings for an alternative to globalization, abolitionists are concerned about the concentration of power within today's international financial institutions. These challengers are particularly disturbed by the BWIs because power within those institutions is not divided equally among states. The Bretton Woods system is viewed by abolitionists as the tool of domination. D.L. Sheth argues:

> Development is now increasingly perceived as a theory not about economic growth and elimination of poverty, but as an ideological and institutional device used by the rich and powerful nations to monitor economic and power relations vis-a-vis the underdeveloped nations in order to maintain the former's political domination and to establish cultural hegemony.[21]

Activists engaged in a process of rejection and delinking are actualizing the theoretical visions of Max-Neef and others. Exemplified by the Chipko movement[22] in India, activists have challenged the legitimacy of the development model by protesting not only its results, but the very process by which their needs are being defined by planners from outside of the local space. They concentrate on satisfying basic human needs, material and non-material, through self-reliance, and they actively resist, through non-violent means, the incursions of development planners in their communities. In practical terms, this translates to a series of familiar community actions: occupying proposed dam sites, tree hugging to protect forests, establishing seed banks and recovering traditional species, resurrecting health-care traditions, and giving equal instruction in practical knowledge and book-learning. In general, the Chipko movement is trying to recapture the local space and resist globalization as modernization.

Many local activists have directly defended their local spaces when the BWIs threaten them. Campaigns originating in Brazil, India, Thailand, Indonesia and Bangladesh have all attracted global attention. In each case, a particular World Bank project has been attacked because it threatens local people and the resources those people depend upon. Similarly, protests from environmentalists and labor unions over the creation of the World Trade Organization (WTO) have arisen from a fear that it will contribute to the ascendancy of the global space over the needs of the local. The IMF is perhaps the most targeted of the institutions. Riots in Jamaica, Sudan, Turkey and other countries have ensued when structural adjustment programs were imposed that were seen as instruments to balance the global economy on the backs of the poor.[23]

CHALLENGING THE CHALLENGERS

Today, as 50 years ago, the world faces the aftermath of a major war, this time the Cold War. In addition, the global economy is in recession. The highest growth rate for any industrialized economy is under 5 per cent. While some countries, notably in South Asia, are experiencing dynamic growth, the social costs of the restructuring programs are high. Many developing countries continue to struggle under excessive levels of debt. Problems in one part of the globe are not isolated incidents any more, for the reality of globalization links the fortunes of all humanity.

Max-Neef considers the structuralist and alternative normative prescriptions to these problems to be mutually exclusive, each requiring a vision of development that excludes the other. The structuralist vision is linear, flowing from correct macroeconomics. The alternative normative approach is systemic, where satisfiers are chosen to meet local needs. The latter view values diversity and self-reliance; the former stresses homogeneity and omnipotence. Both views extend the concept of equitable, sustainable and participatory development beyond the borders of the developing countries, but both also have limitations.

The obvious limitation of the structuralist prescription is its lack of participatory mechanisms. New global institutions are likely to carry the same structural flaws as the current BWIs unless a mechanism is found to separate them from the source of their legitimacy, the states. This is exactly what most structuralists dream of – institutions which are no longer hampered by national interests. Removing the control mechanisms that industrialized states now use to manipulate the BWIs would free them to act for the greater good. But even if it were possible to create institutions free from state interests, which is unlikely, one can wonder if it is desirable. Global economics would become entrusted to bureaucrats (most likely schooled in the banking tradition) who would be unaccountable to any constituency, state or otherwise. This would, of course, make a mockery of democracy. It would also leave the world's people at the mercy of a handful of individuals accountable to no one. One is reminded of the old saying, 'Power corrupts and absolute power corrupts absolutely.' The reformist economists do not address this power question, considering it outside the realm of economics. But economics as practised by the BWIs has included any social issue which requires an aggregate response, such as health, environment, labor and education. In fact, the only issue which has thus far been safe from the reach of economics is religion. There is no reason to believe that new institutions would not encompass the same broad cross-section of societal concerns.

The second major question, related to the first, is the question of legitimacy. Compliance would obviously require coercion, meaning that the institutions would need more than a fair amount of power. From where would they derive this power? And how would it relate to the local space, the right to self-determination and democratic principles? Only one structuralist has seriously addressed these questions. David Held advocates new supranational institutions which include only democratic states.[24] This solution, however, has its own limitation. Capital knows no boundaries and therefore would not be controlled by institutions which are not all-inclusive. Second, Held recognizes various definitions of democracy, but does not provide a solution for the inevitable power struggle over adopting a definition. The prevailing Western view of democracy as representation would likely become definitive, precluding other definitions, such as the direct democracy prevalent in the Greek city-state. Iran, for example, where every citizen has the right to vote from age 16, would most likely not be recognized as a democratic state. Finally, although states are not the only players on the global scene, few structuralists have grappled with the mechanisms necessary to include non-state actors in global decision making.[25] Reform-minded economists have not faced up to this problem. Unless and until the structuralist challengers grapple with the need for mechanisms for participation and accountability to be embedded in supranational structures, they will fall short of the goal of participatory, sustainable and equitable development.

While the alternative normative challengers have done a better job of addressing the power question, the confederated approach of their development process falls short when it reaches the level of interaction among local spaces. No prescriptions are provided for the borders of each local space. The extrapolated vision might resemble the political structure of the canton system in Switzerland on a global level. However, one has to imagine this, because the visions put forth by this group never leave the local space. They do not, for example, offer prescriptions for controlling global capital. They adopt the defensive posture of self-realization, which would give communities the necessary tools to block a supranational decision-making process which does not have their best interests at heart.

CONCLUSION

Fusing the strengths of these two visions of a new international economic order would result in an arrangement far superior to that of the current BWIs. This is the challenge that must be undertaken in order to traverse the next 50 years with global peace and prosperity. The search continues for a global structure of institutions which can correct the imbalances of a globalized economy for the benefit of all citizens without undermining democracy, while allowing sufficient space for creative and diverse forms of economy on the local level. Various fora, such as the Rethinking Bretton Woods Conference, the UN World Summit for Social Development, the North–South Roundtable, the G–7 and others, are taking up the challenge of crafting global institutions for the twenty-first century that incorporate both the structuralist and the alternative normative Bretton Woods challengers.

Notes

1. Two of the works used by the project to stimulate debate were: Walter Russell Mead, 'American Economic Policy in the Antemillennial Era' in *World Policy Journal*, vol. 6, no. 3, 1989, pp. 385–468; and United Nations Development Programme, *Human Development Report 1992* (New York: Oxford University Press, 1992).
2. Manfred Max-Neef, 'Development and Human Needs' in M. Max-Neef and P. Ekins (eds), *Real Life Economics: Understanding Wealth Creation* (London: Routledge, 1992)
3. George Aditjondro, 'A Reflection about Past International Advocacy Work on Indonesian Environmental Issues' (mimeo, 1990).
4. Vandana Shiva is an Indian feminist and ecologist. Trained in nuclear physics, she was dismayed by her colleagues' lack of concern for the ecological and health implications of nuclear radiation, and

turned her attention to science and technology policy. She has written widely on issues of gender, ecology, development and trade, and in 1993 received the Swedish Right Livelihood Award, also known as the Alternate Nobel Prize. See 'Beware the Backlash' in *The Guardian*, March 11, 1994, p. 16; 'From Adjustment to Sustainable Development, the Obstacle of Free Trade' in Ralph Nader *et al.*, *The Case Against Free Trade: GATT, NAFTA and the Globalization of Corporate Power* (San Francisco: Earth Island Press, 1993); *Close to Home: Women Reconnect Ecology, Health and Development* (Philadelphia: New Society Publishers, 1994); and, with Maria Mies, *Ecofeminism* (London: Zed Books, 1993).

5. The '50 Years is Enough' campaign calls for:

> [t]he full participation of affected men and women in all aspects of World Bank and IMF projects, policies, and programs. This will require far-reaching changes in the lending policies, internal processes and structure of the World Bank and the IMF. Only when these reforms are implemented will these institutions be able to play a positive role in support of equitable, sustainable development.

50 Years is Enough Campaign, 'Campaign Platform' (Washington, DC: 50 Years is Enough, 1994). This document was the joint effort of several member organizations of the campaign. For more information, see: Danaher, Kevin (ed.), *50 Years is Enough: The Case Against the World Bank and the International Monetary Fund* (Boston, MA: South End Press, 1994).

6. See Chapter 1 of this volume: Sixto K. Roxas, 'Principles for Institutional Reform'.

7. Mead, 'American Economic Policy'.

8. UNDP, *Human Development Report 1992*.

9. Mead, 'American Economic Policy', p. 425.

10. UNDP, *Human Development Report 1992*, pp. 75–9.

11. Mead, 'American Economic Policy', pp. 427, 429.

12. Mead, p. 434.

13. UNDP, *Human Development Report 1992*, p. 79.

14. For details, see D.L. Sheth, 'Alternative Development as Political Practice' in *Alternatives*, vol. XII, no. 2, 1987, p. 158.

15. Max-Neef, 'Development and Human Needs', p. 212.

16. Max-Neef, p. 202.

17. Max-Neef, p. 198.

18. Max-Neef, p. 21 Max-Neef writes about Latin America. Ronald Inglehart tracks a similar phenomenon in industrialized society, where the supremacy of production and quantity is slowly being rejected for social issues. See Inglehart's *Culture Shift in Advanced Industrial Society* (Princeton, NJ: Princeton University Press, 1990).

19. Aditjondro, 'A Reflection', p. 12.
20. Aditjondro, p. 13.
21. Sheth, 'Alternative Development', p. 156.
22. Chipko is the forest protection movement that began in the early 1970s in India's Garhwal Hills, in the foothills of the Himalaya mountains. Chipko, which means 'to embrace', takes its name from a village protest when people hugged trees to prevent logging. By a leading Chipko activist, Sunderlal Bahuguna, see *Echoes from the Hills: Save the Himalayan Eco-System: A Call to Humanity* (New Delhi: New Age Printing Press, 1992) and *Whither Development? Chipko Message, 1994* (Silgara, India: Chipko Information Center, 1994). Also see: Robert A. Hutchinson, 'Sunderlal Bahuguna and the Chipko Movement' in *Smithsonian*, vol. 18, no. 11 (February 1988) pp. 184–90; and Brian Nelson, 'Chipko Revisited' in *Whole Earth Review*, no. 79 (June 22, 1993) pp. 116–21.
23. See Kavaljit Singh and Dalip Swamy, *Against Consensus: Three Years of Public Resistance to Structural Adjustment Program* (Delhi: Public Interest Research Group, 1994); and Kenneth S. Smith, 'World Bank, IMF – Do They Help or Hurt Third World?' in *US News and World Report*, April 29, 1985, pp. 43–6.
24. David Held, 'Democracy: From City States to a Cosmopolitan Order?' in *Political Studies*, vol. XL, Special Issue: Prospects for Democracy, 1992, pp. 10–39.
25. For a discussion of this point, see Daniel D. Bradlow and Claudio Grossman in Chapter 2 of this volume, 'Adjusting the Bretton Woods Institutions to Contemporary Realities'.

5. The New Development Paradigm: Organizing for Implementation

Turid Sato and William E. Smith[1]

INTRODUCTION

In September 1993, ten countries sent delegations representing their governments, non-governmental organizations, the private sector and academic communities to discuss implementing a new development paradigm with representatives from development assistance agencies. At the request of the project's sponsors – the governments of Japan and the Netherlands and the United Nations Development Programme (UNDP) – the project organizer, Organizing for Development, an International Institute (ODII), prepared a workshop report, on which this chapter is based.

ORIGIN OF THE PROJECT

The inspiration for the project emerged from the many reviews, discussions and white papers – in Japan, Europe, Africa, Latin America and the United States – which evaluated the results of four decades of development assistance. There was broad agreement that the current system, having accumulated some $1.5 trillion in debt, has not produced results commensurate with the resources expended. Disillusioned with the results, many development practitioners and institutions are actively exploring new and more appropriate approaches to development by which much more can be done for much less.

Initial support for the idea of exploring a new development paradigm came from the Norwegian Agency for Development Cooperation (NORAD). Having critically reviewed its own philosophy and strategy for development, NORAD was already beginning to turn away from its donor-driven approach. It knew that it must encourage self-help, self-reliance and empowerment. However, such strategies would not work if they were not supported by other development agencies and governments. A global workshop offered the possibility of developing more consensus on new paradigms.

Japanese officials supported a workshop to allow diverse cultures to come together to explore the implications of such a development paradigm. The Netherlands and the UNDP also became project sponsors.

'The New Development Paradigm' applies to development work the qualitative changes that have already taken place in other fields. Thomas Kuhn, in his book *The Structure of Scientific Revolutions*, helped to popularize the term 'paradigm'. While popular usage has come to interpret a paradigm as simply a 'world view', Kuhn's definition of a paradigm is more precise: 'Universally recognized scientific achievements that for a time provide model problems and solutions to a community of practitioners.'[2] Kuhn used the term paradigm in relation to the tremendous shift in the scientific worldview, from the mechanistic approach of Newton to the relativistic one of Einstein. In the political world, the new paradigm has created a vortex of change swirling from eastern Europe, dismantling the Soviet Union, and bringing rumbles of democratic change through Asia, Africa and Latin America.

A paradigm shift in development, to be minimally consistent with Kuhn's concept, would need to meet three conditions:

1. It must provide a meta-theory, that is, one that serves to explain many other theories.

2. It must be accepted by a community of practitioners.

3. It must have a body of successful practice, 'exemplars', that are held up as 'paradigms' in practice.

If there is indeed a new development paradigm, then:

• What is the meta-theory?

• Who is the community?

• What are the successful exemplars?

• Who has made and who has yet to make the shift?

PURPOSE

The first specific purpose of the 1993 workshop on development was to communicate the ideals, practices and implications of the 'New Development Paradigm' to a broad, cross-cultural sector of the development community that includes many cultures. The defining trait of the new development paradigm was that development must be human-centered, coming from within, rather than imposed from the outside. In addition, the center of effort in development needs to shift from resource-based strategies to interactive or participative strategies. In many ways, local practitioners are far ahead of the international donor agencies and the recipient governments.[3]

Second, the intention was to provide an opportunity for country teams engaged in programs consistent with the ideals of the new paradigm to learn from each other and to help translate these ideals into practical applications that could serve as exemplars. In order to conduct future development work consistent with the new paradigm, three strategic clusters of questions needed to be addressed:

1. how to design learning institutions and processes that could change the attitude and mindsets of those still caught in the old paradigm;

2. how to ensure the necessary shifts in priorities, roles and responsibilities that would produce more holistic, sustainable development, and

3. how to ensure financial support for the use of democratic processes for full involvement.

Finally, the project attempted to open a new dialogue between donor institutions and developing countries to encourage a new pattern of relationships more consistent with the requirements of the new development paradigm. Many development assistance institutions find it difficult 'to let go of the rope', wishing to control the outputs and the terms of interaction between stakeholders. The costs of this reluctance to change in terms of administration and the destruction of initiative are enormous.

The Meta-theory

There was clear acceptance that development should be people-centered; democratically organized; responsive to the whole environment, not only the ecological and the economic, but also the political, social, and cultural; and balanced, for example, between center and periphery, between public and private, between the roles of men and women. Development was described as an increase in one's capacity to pursue purposes, while taking into account the effects of achieving that purpose on others and on the whole community. The achievement of human purpose becomes the goal of development, the touchstone against which development is assessed.

The new development paradigm puts human purpose at the center as the driving force or source of power for development. It draws on all human values – social, political, aesthetic and spiritual, as well as the economic and scientific – as criteria for success. This philosophy differs considerably from that driving the development paradigm of the last four decades. The stories told by the participants showed how unreal and how costly the former analysis from the outside has proven to be. The story of the Grameen Bank, in contrast, reveals what can be done when human purpose is placed at the center and supported by interaction among peers (see 'Grameen Bank' in Glossary). This new philosophy enables much more to be accomplished for much less.

Visualizing the Meta-theory

Building on the visual presentation of the ideals in Figure 5.1, the new development paradigm is illustrated in Figure 5.2, which encompasses and synthesizes these ideals. The image extends the organizing principle used to construct Figure 5.1.

The new paradigm is organized around the three fundamental systems' relationships:

1. the relationship to the whole system (in this case identified as the circle containing the scientific, spiritual, social, political, economic and ecological context of development);

2. the relationships among the parts of the system (in this case the organizations, agencies and institutions involved in development), and

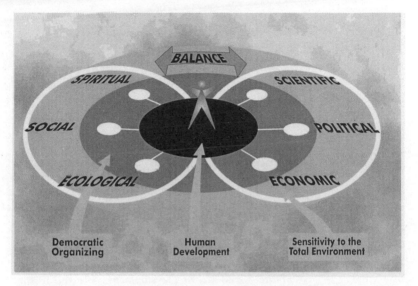

Figure 5.1 The Ideals of the New Development Paradigm

3. the relationship of the individual part to itself (in this case the individual or organization acting as part of the development system).

The essence of each relationship consists in different forms of power:

- *appreciation* of the whole – understanding the realities and the potential inherent in the whole system;

- *influence* of and among the parts – determination of which part has priority and what the relationships among the parts should be, and

- *control* of the individual part – the autonomy of the individual part and the resources it possesses.

It can be concluded that the traditional model of development is based on control. It is assumed that underdevelopment is caused by lack of resources, technology and skills. The remedy, governed pri-

93

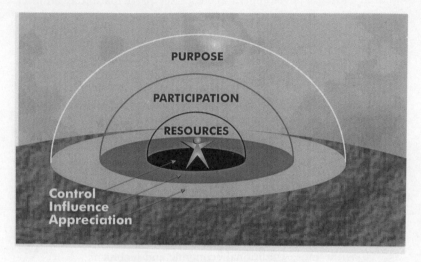

Figure 5.2 Model of Development

marily by economic values, is to transfer the missing resources from the developed to the developing world. The failures of this strategy are myriad. For example, an overemphasis on control has led to the over-bureaucratization of development and to the fragmentation of development efforts into small projects with high overhead costs and little coordination in relationship to the whole country. There are frequent 'disconnects' in traditional development projects and in many projects carried out by different departments or entities, often pursuing opposite goals. The effect is one of 'winning the battle but losing the war', that is, the immediate goal may be reached, but the overall purpose is not advanced.

This failure points to the need to move to the second level, labeled 'participation' in Figure 5.2. Characterized by exchange of influence among the stakeholders (the parts) of the development system, this level determines who sets development priorities, and what roles different parties (stakeholders) should play. In the traditional model, the primary interaction is among experts. Experts decide priorities and design the structures which determine roles and relationships. Often those who have most influence on successful implementation are not party to the design, management or evaluation of development programs.

Staff of many development agencies see participation as another implementing technology – a sub-component of resource allocation, and one with which they are quite uncomfortable. A typical positive response by the agencies to the requirement for more participation is to increase training programs and produce guidelines and handbooks to teach the new techniques of participation. This approach totally misses the point. Participation is not just another implementing technology; it represents a whole new philosophy of development that leads to new policies, new roles and new relationships. Participation is the strategic centerpiece of a new model and a new philosophy of development. It is also more democratic than the current top-down model of development. This leads to questions about the third level of the model.

What is the purpose of development? Different interpretations of the purpose are based on different philosophies and lead to different models and practices. To be effective, development must address the long-term needs of the whole community; it must include all aspects of development – political, social and cultural, as well as the more traditional economic and technical.

The new model of development shifts the center of effort from a focus on control of resources to the participative dimension, the interaction among the key parts of the development system. It is driven by the purpose of the stakeholders rather than by expert planning.

The Community of Practitioners and Some Exemplars

Because much of the search for improved practices of development over the last four decades has concentrated on better mechanisms of control, attention needs to shift to practices that lead to greater appreciation and greater influence.

Thailand's 'Five Star Partnership Program' provides a dramatic illustration of such new practices. To implement the new development paradigm, the government of Thailand has entered into a partnership with the NGO community, the private sector, academic and religious organizations in the form of the Thai Foundation. The main purposes of the Thai Foundation in promoting this 'five star partnership' are: to facilitate a process in which villages, districts, and provinces establish their own priorities in the context of the realities and potential that exist; and to encourage the formation of similar partnerships at the local level to help in the implementation of those priorities.

95

The key elements of their practice were:

* change of attitudes through learning (appreciation);

* working together with the help of facilitative processes (influence), and

* involving people in improving their own lives and their own environment (control).

Thailand's new paradigm exemplar has features that are essential for successful implementation. First, people are not expected to switch to new paradigm practices without a change in attitude or mindset. Some experiential learning processes are required to produce such changes. The role of the national organization, the Thai Foundation, is to promote these facilitative processes.

Second, participation is required across projects and programs to meet the needs of whole districts, whole provinces or the whole nation. Participation of many parties requires strengthening of coordinative mechanisms. The Thai partnership concept represents a coordinative mechanism at the national level. They also call for a similar system at each level, each providing a learning, a facilitative and a funding function for learning and facilitation for the level below. The relationship between the three levels is governed not by control or bureaucratic norms, but by influence and appreciative relationships. Government of higher-level systems creates the conditions for private parties and organizations to appreciate their impact on the whole, partnerships are used to create constructively cooperative and appropriately competitive relationships among the parts of the whole system.

Third, within this field of appreciation and influence, individual organizations and communities are free to make their own decisions and to take responsibility for their own actions.

The most well-known case is the Grameen Bank in Bangladesh, which has appealed to the purpose of development (appreciative power) and social pressures (influence powers) to ensure repayment of loans at a higher level than almost any other development bank. For borrowers, initial credit is not contingent on collateral (control), and future credit depends on repayment performance.

RECOMMENDATIONS FOR DEVELOPMENT INSTITUTIONS

The paradigm shift now overtaking practitioners of development has major implications at each of the three levels:

1. Appreciation: What is the purpose of development institutions? Is this purpose congruent with current realities and opportunities? What is the current mindset of the leadership o
emerging paradigm? What is the mindset needed for the new development paradigm?

2. I
institutions to other stakeholders in the development system, for example, the private sector, NGOs and local communities?

3. Control: What are the core processes used by development agencies? Are they appropriate for implementing the new paradigm of development? Are the selection and development of human, financial and informational resources appropriate to the new models?

Improving Appreciation

There are numerous ways to improve the appreciation of the whole system and change old attitudes toward the development process, including:

- involve leadership of development agencies in Search Conferences to support new purposes, models and practices;

- extend the Thai idea of a National Institute to facilitate new paradigm processes at the global level;

- support cross-cultural programs and exchanges with countries practicing new paradigm approaches. Focus on women and youth in particular;

- create institutional support for facilitation of democratic organizing processes for sustainable development;

- create a dynamic media strategy and support for the free press, and broadcast, televise and publicize exemplars of the new philosophy in action.

Improving Influence

To improve the influence of those people most affected by the decisions taken, the following steps are recommended:

- Increase participation of women. This will automatically shift priorities, roles and relationships towards more appreciative values which are part of the new paradigm.

- Increase participation of all those with a stake in development through democratic processes and institutions.

- Create competition between existing institutions by giving organizations and countries access to new forms of assistance that will support partnerships and learning processes.

- Create new partnerships at national levels among governments, the private sector and NGOs.

- At the regional and local levels, create partnerships among governments, private sector, NGOs and local communities.

- Modify the role of the multilateral development banks to more closely fit their financial expertise and to reduce the conflict of interest involved in their role in the selection, design and preparation of projects.

- Modify the role of UNDP to ensure that it emphasizes its coordinative rather than project preparation role. This implies a major shift away from selecting and preparing projects to one of strengthening the facilitative role of government in support of partnerships between governments, the private sector and NGOs and of sustainable development. UNDP's support for technical assistance should be offered only as a last resort after all local resources and skills have been exhausted.

Improving Peoples' Control

Several concrete steps can be taken to ensure more effective peoples' control over their own development and their own environment:

- Give greater emphasis in planning and implementation to dealing with problems and programs holistically – involve whole organizations, whole villages, whole provinces and whole regions in the design and implementation process.

- Decentralize control of programs to levels that can take a holistic perspective and give them control of resources and responsibility for managing the whole, rather than continue to micro-manage development from the top.

- Redesign the project selection and planning processes of the development agencies in the light of participative principles.

- Shift the emphasis of development interventions from analysis and report writing to interaction and commitment to action.

- Make evaluation the first, rather than the last, step of the organizing process; make appraisal an ongoing process to be carried out by the stakeholders; and make monitoring part of a self-managing process carried out by the implementers.

- Select and reward staff for greater breadth of understanding of development. Encourage more flexible and less controlling relationships between development agency staff and clients.

- Create new funding mechanisms that would encourage broader, more transparent and flexible planning, budgeting and accounting procedures.

NEXT STEPS

ODII plans to engage the leadership of the development agencies, governments, and implementing organizations in an ongoing dialogue about progress in implementing the new development paradigm. It plans to test the degree of interest in creating a 'development facility' to support implementation of the new development paradigm at the global level involving a partnership of interested donors and recipient governments, the private sector, NGOs and academic and religious organizations.

Modeled on the Thai Foundation, the function of this facility would be to provide the leadership of the global development community with the support required to shift to the new paradigm, to identify constraints that exist in the existing development frameworks and to meet the learning needs of practitioners of new paradigm approaches. The 50th anniversary of the Bretton Woods institutions offered a symbolic time for the initiation of such an effort.

ODII will encourage countries planning to create similar facilitative foundations and programs to link their experiences to such an international learning and co-creation process and join in its creation. At the local level, ODII plans to extend its transcultural experience into the local community of Washington, DC and other US communities, thereby reconfirming the end of the distinction between the First, Second and Third Worlds and recognizing that we are only one developing world.

CONCLUSION

The wave created by the new paradigm in science, in politics, and now in development, has reached tidal proportions. Kuhn has explained that people do not accept new paradigms through arguments and reason. The switch is made through experiencing the new phenomenon; it is made all at once or not at all. Paradigms are wholes that are, according to Kuhn, 'incommensurable'. One must 'fight or switch', and the time to fight is over.

The Thai experience provides a true exemplar of the new paradigm. It encompasses the 'purpose' or 'appreciative' dimension by drawing on the spiritual traditions of Buddhism. It proposes the spread of this new philosophy through the creation of a facilitative organization (the Thai Foundation) ensuring that it meets the needs of the whole Thai community. It conceptualizes and has started to implement the participative 'influence' dimension through its Five Star Partnership of government, private sector, religious organizations, grassroots organization, and academic institutions. It has ensured that its resource based programs, at the local level, themselves became centers of development, each containing the whole spirit and participative model of the new philosophy.

The major challenge of the new development paradigm is to

shift the emphasis of development assistance to a higher plane – from a focus on resources to a focus on human purpose and interaction. In practice, it means changing the mindset of those who still see participation or interaction as methodology. It means developing new structures and processes that will identify and facilitate interaction among the key stakeholders of the development system. It means creating new financial mechanisms that can respond to the needs generated by such a process rather than being tied *a priori* to the financiers' view of development needs.

There are many cases in which such constraints had been overcome, and many others where such efforts continue to be undermined. The biggest obstacles to the implementation of such ideas have been institutionalized attitudes, patterns of relationship, and core processes that are based on the philosophy that sees development as expertise to be transferred along with technology and financial resources.

The governments, development agencies and other bureaucracies holding on to the resource philosophy fear that the move into a more participative mode will mean loss of control. The cases of success show admirably that the opposite is true: 'letting go of the rope' can lead to more power. As Halle Jorn Hanssen of Norway asserted: 'Governments and development agencies have to learn to operate with more appreciation and influence and less control.'[4] If they do not, they are likely to end up in the same predicament as many of the controlling institutions in eastern Europe and the former Soviet Union, existing without a purpose and, eventually, without resources.

On a hopeful note, many governments and the development agencies are becoming aware of the new ideas. Although lack of support, and even sabotage, of such new efforts are still too common, many practitioners feel that a new climate has already been created that encourages experimentation with new models, strategies and practices. A change of attitude is taking place.

Human-centered development, then, requires a shift in the center of development effort – one which is inspired from within rather than imposed from without – one which empowers, rather than disempowers. Human-centered development cannot be achieved by gradual changes or improvements in methodology. Human-centered development requires a whole new attitude and philosophy, new models and new practices, and new roles for governments and for development assistance agencies.

Human-centered development requires a change in attitude. Each of us is that human being at the center of the development model in Figures 5.1 and 5.2. None is the skin-bounded self, but the self which includes relationships to others and to the whole. Whether as individual practitioners, or as whole organizations or governments, all are responsible for the effect of our actions on others and the whole. All are collectively responsible for the current mess in the development domain. All share the responsibility to improve it.

Notes

1. The authors are co-directors of Organizing for Development, an International Institute (ODII), which they helped to found in 1988. This chapter is based on the report they prepared for the sponsors of ODII's September 1993 workshop on implementing the new development paradigm.
2. Thomas Kuhn, *The Structure of Scientific Revolutions* (Chicago: University of Chicago Press, 1962 and 1970), preface to the second edition, p. viii.
3. For greater detail, see ODII's 1994 report, *The Magic of Interaction* (Washington, DC: ODII, 1994).
4. Halle Jorn Hanssen at the ODII Workshop on the New Development Paradigm, at the Airlie Center in Virginia, September 8–11, 1993.

6. Changing Paradigms and Indicators: Implementing Equitable, Sustainable and Participatory Development

Hazel Henderson

INTRODUCTION

Underlying the rethinking of the Bretton Woods institutions (BWIs) is a fundamental shift toward a new development paradigm. The 1987 report of the World Commission on Environment and Development, *Our Common Future*, which spread and popularized the concept of 'sustainable development', defined it as 'development which meets the needs of the present without compromising the ability of future generations to meet their own needs'.[1] UN Secretary General Boutros Boutros-Ghali emphasized in his May 1994 *Agenda for Development* that the focus of the United Nations on sustainable development was even more important than its peacekeeping mission: 'Without development there is no prospect for lasting peace.' He added, 'Moreover, the allocation of resources between various dimensions of development remains unbalanced ... Many activities, especially in the area of social development, remain underfinanced.'[2]

In this paradigm shift, debates rage over old paradigm contradictions and anomalies; what to measure and how to measure it; and how to treat those services, amenities, values and resources which have no price. This comprehensive rethinking of underlying premises embraces far more than the Bretton Woods institutions: it questions long-held beliefs about money, wealth, productivity, efficiency, and progress itself.[3] Neoclassical economics, as embraced by the Bretton Woods institutions, diverges from other

103

GNP "Private" Sector rests on → GNP "Public" Sector which rests on → Social Cooperative Counter-Economy which rests on → Nature's Layer

Official Market Economy
All Cash Transactions

"Private" Sector Production, employment, consumption, investment, savings

"Public" Sector Infrastructure (roads, maintenance, sewers, bridges, subways, schools, municipal government) Defense, state and local gov't.

Cash-Based "Underground economy" tax dodges

"Sweat-Equity": Do-it-yourself, bartering social, family, community structures, unpaid household & parenting, volunteering, sharing, mutual aid, caring for old and sick, home-based production for use, subsistence agriculture

Mother Nature Natural resource base - absorbs costs of pollution, recycles wastes if tolerances not exceeded, GNP sectors "external" costs hidden (toxic dumps, etc.)

GNP-Monetized 1/2 of Cake

Top two layers
Monetized, officially measured GNP generates all economic statistics (15% "underground" illegal, tax-dodging)

Non-Monetized Productive 1/2 of Cake

Lower two layers
Non-monetized altruism, sharing "counter-economy" subsidizes top two GNP-cash sectors with unpaid labor and environmental costs absorbed or unaccounted, risks passed to future generations

economics in that its body of thought evolved to rationalize and support the mechanisms of the industrial revolution that began in Britain about 300 years ago. Adam Smith described the emerging proliferation of free markets with unabashed approval: as he saw it, social progress could at last be achieved based on human *frailties* – acquisitiveness, greed and self-centeredness – rather than waiting until human beings perfected themselves. Markets allocate resources with unmatched efficiency when Adam Smith's conditions – that buyers and sellers negotiate in these markets with equal power and information, while harming no unrelated parties – are met.[4]

The shift from concern with economic growth, as measured by per capita averaged Gross National Product (GNP), toward equitable, sustainable and participatory development, demands new indicators and criteria to measure efforts and results. The high costs of GNP growth, from environmental degradation to cultural and community disruption, are now obvious. Biologists and ecologists have been sounding the alarm since Rachel Carson wrote *Silent Spring* in 1962,[5] but these warnings were largely ignored because textbook economics assumed that environmental resources were either unlimited or plentiful enough to be omitted from GNP accounts.

The concept of a difference between Gross Domestic Product (GDP) and GNP was introduced into the national accounting systems of the United States, the United Kingdom and their allies during World War II to recognize war production by domestically-owned factories operating outside the country. After 1945, GNP and GDP continued to assess bombs and bullets highly, while setting at zero the worth of infrastructure, education, health, and environmental assets. Also ignored was the approximately 50 per cent of production, even in industrial countries, that is unpaid, such as do-it-yourself home construction and maintenance, food production for one's own household, caring for family members, and volunteer hours (89 million American adults do volunteer work at least five hours a week, saving substantial costs in government social services). (See Figure 6.1.)

Opposite.
Figure 6.1 Total Productive System of an Industrial Society
(Copyright © 1982 Hazel Henderson)

PARADIGM DEBATES

Values and Indicators

The role of social and environmental indicators became a focus of attention after the UN Conference on Environment and Development (UNCED) in Rio de Janeiro, 1992. Rio's *Agenda 21* commits all 178 signatory countries to expand their national statistical accounts by including both environmental factors and unpaid work.[6] New measuring rods, the subject of hot debate over the past decade, are now emerging. The United Nations Commission on Sustainable Development (UNCSD), formed to follow up on the implementation of *Agenda 21*, will monitor efforts to integrate sustainability criteria and data into national accounting, corporate balance sheets and economic theory under the expert eye of Nitin Desai, the United Nations' new Undersecretary General for Policy Coordination and Sustainable Development. Such panels on statistical instruments, for better or worse, guide governments, enterprises, institutions and, when amplified in the mass media, most societal decisions.

Statistics are never value free, however objective or accurate. They incorporate worldviews, goals and social values: those unique 'cultural DNA codes' that underlie societies, their traditions and visions for the future.[7] And although economics parades itself as value free, even as a science, it clearly does not represent an objective search for truth. While no discipline is truly objective, some, such as physics or engineering, can produce repeatable results and reliable techniques. Economics is a profession with little quality control. Economists are like lawyers in that an economic cost–benefit analysis is an advocacy-oriented document similar to a lawyer's brief; designed to marshal arguments and data to support programs that clients (governments, BWIs or corporations) wish to promote. Economics is a 300 year-old grab-bag of non-verifiable and non-refutable hypotheses parading as principles. As this author has pointed out,[8] economists solemnly cite beliefs like Alfred Marshall's Principles of Economics and Vilfredo Pareto's Optimality Principle, as if they were analogous to verifiable physical principles such as Newton's Laws of Motion. The difference is clear: physical laws can guide spacecraft to moon landings, whereas economic principles are little more than hypotheses, or worse, the thinly disguised norms of economists themselves.

Much is at stake for economists if they are forced to admit that their development prescriptions have been too narrowly conceived. Within these contexts we must consider how traditional statistics and the System of National Accounts (SNA) can be usefully related to emerging social and environmental indicators. Further, these new indicators must also mesh with the BWIs and other government and private institutions, not just at micro- and macro-economic levels, but at global levels where new regulatory systems, standards and international agreements need to be developed and harmonized.

The backdrop for the debates is today's largely *ad hoc* world financial economy which has greatly expanded as a result of the internationalization of industrialism, technology and information, and the long-term global functioning of the United Nations and the BWIs. This globalized economic apparatus with the daily turnover of $1 trillion on foreign exchange markets worldwide[9] swamps real investment and trade, and drives most other institutions, policies and activities. It has facilitated the successful spread of industrialism and industrialism's second-order effects: the marginalization of traditional societies and cultures; restructuring of work and production; widening of poverty gaps; increasing pollution, and unsustainable levels of consumption and waste. Thus, development imperatives for the future must focus on redirecting the world economic game toward sustainable development, changing the current rules and scorecards of the game, that is, per capita economic growth measured by GDP.

Problems with the Old Paradigm

There is growing concern about GDP growth policies that widen poverty gaps and exacerbate unemployment. Indeed, jobless economic growth is increasing around the world, as described in the *Human Development Report 1993* of the United Nations Development Programme (UNDP). Jobless economic growth is the result of the focus on industrialization and a narrowly conceived view of production efficiency. Productivity statistics in terms of per capita averages still focus on labor, driving economies toward greater emphasis on capital and mechanization, even as politicians promise full employment. Non-economists point out that this focus is contradictory, ignores externalities, and increases unemployment. A generation of economists have devoted themselves to elaborating cases in which job creation in new enterprises has, over time, filled the gap. These studies are used by corporations and investors to lobby for more generous investment tax credits, justified to spur job creation. While many government officials understand that technological changes displace jobs, they rely on the hypothesis that GDP growth and technological progress will re-employ those displaced. The economists' recipe for GDP-measured growth, using narrow production-efficiency statistics, disregards social and environmental costs. It cannibalizes social and environmental productivity (see Figure 6.1), leading to fewer workers with more sophisticated tools producing more goods and services, while unemployment and welfare rolls grow. In a burst of enthusiastic orthodoxy, *The Economist*, in a February 1993 editorial, actually hailed the jobless economic growth syndrome as 'the Holy Grail of economic prosperity'.[10]

This purely economic formula for industrial progress, productivity, and global competitiveness impacts first on agriculture, shifting workers from their land to urban areas and factories, then as factories automate, workers move to the services sector – today's vaunted 'information society'. They must be constantly retrained for new, more sophisticated tasks that, textbook models assume, will reliably increase to employ those displaced by automation. And a steady stream of people in search of jobs in overpopulated cities swell the migration from sustainable rural communities. This scenario is now playing out on a global stage, with unexpected and appalling results: the service sectors are also automating and corporations, to stay competitive, roam the world in search of cheap labor and unprotected resources. Companies downsize middle-management and part-time their work force to shed fringe benefits, while continuing to automate factory and office work. Even *The Economist* now agrees that 'technology has, so far, played a bigger role than trade in increasing wage inequality'.[11]

The North American Free Trade Agreement (NAFTA) debate, 'conducted in terms of fallacies exposed 150 years ago',[12] was a prelude to the global scramble for cheaper labor and its flip side: increased migration as workers follow capital flows and potential jobs across national borders. The forces of globalization have invalidated the economic textbooks and statistics that still assume there are national economies with capital and labor remaining relatively stationary within their borders.

Today, Organization for Economic Cooperation and Development (OECD) countries face new dilemmas: creeping budget deficits and jobless growth are the symptoms, but old remedies no longer apply. As economies pick up and jobs are restored, global bond traders speculating between long- and short-term interest rates start worrying about inflation. The so-called Non-Accelerating Inflation Rate of Unemployment (NAIRU) signals inflation whenever unemployment rates decrease. The slightest hint that the Loch Ness monster of inflation has been sighted throws central bank policies and financial markets into reverse. However, trying to strangle inflation with high interest rates chokes off the growth, jobs and consumer spending on which economies rely, and sends a multiplier shock back to the consumer price index in a vicious circle. The concept of NAIRU is now under attack for signaling non-existent inflationary pressures and determining that a 7 per cent jobless rate equals 'full employment'. That figure has been creeping up from the 2 per cent of decades ago, as job creation targets have been missed. Worse, as President Clinton has learned, rising government debt and deficit preclude the time-honored Keynesian tools of stimulus and pump-priming deficit spending.

At the March 1994 Jobs Summit in the United States, leaders of the Group of Seven (G–7), the major industrial nations, avoided the issues that underlie joblessness. They did not face new fundamentals: the unchecked forces of globalization, the exhaustion of the industrial growth recipe itself, and the outdated productivity and competitiveness formulas of a generation of economists relying too heavily on obsolete models and macrostatistics. As yet, few world leaders realize that their way out of today's cul-de-sac is to redirect policy toward a sustainable development paradigm that uses productivity and environmental efficiency criteria to integrate economic and social development.

Instead, G–7 ministers continued backing into the future; deregulating labor markets to make them more 'flexible' and emphasizing more and better jobs training. Making labor markets more flexible translates into calls for dismantling safety nets by limiting fringe benefits, minimum wages and social programs. Training was hailed as a good thing, but few could explain how it would help workers in the face of a shrinking job base. Millions of Americans with college degrees are underemployed in low-wage or part-time jobs; such statistical illusions as counting any job that offers 20-hours a week or more as full-time, lead to false complacency. One pre-1980s 40-hour-a-week job now is often divided into two 20-hour a week jobs. Economists who reviewed the Jobs Summit regarded part-time jobs as a 'preference', but they can hardly call it that for job seekers who are dropped from unemployment figures without full employment. No wonder countries in the South are questioning traditional Western models and indicators of progress.[13]

The Detroit Jobs Summit targeted 'structural joblessness' issues, such as health costs, aging populations and inefficient labor markets. Such old paradigm views also target safety-net legislation, and blame fringe benefits and minimum wages, rather than automation-favoring investment tax credits, for pricing labor out of markets. Yet in the United States, average total compensation (including fringe benefits) is *lower* in real terms than in 1987.[14] The real problem, buried in a *Business Week* article, is the relative cost of labor *vis-a-vis* capital, a relationship exacerbated by productivity formulas and tax incentives.[15] In a global economy investors can roam the world rather than create domestic jobs that will require employment taxes. By using full-cost prices for energy and virgin raw materials and applying value-extracted taxes (VET), a more ecologically and actuarially correct levy than the European value-added taxes (VAT), to discourage waste and pollution, economies can run on a leaner mix of capital, energy and materials, and a richer mix of human resources. Such basic shifts will direct economies toward sustainability, resource efficiency *and* fuller employment – even if the new jobs will be in pollution control and environmental cleanup, or in developing renewable energy sources and efficient green technologies.

The leaders of the OECD may be forced to face these facts, since there is no way out of the present economic impasse without a reformulation of NAIRU and other employment indicators. The G–7 countries (except for Japan, which has a different set of problems) are saddled with rising budget deficits that the OECD's 1993 *Economic Outlook* warns are increasingly structural. Although these problems signal the need for a paradigm shift, which implies a major overhaul of orthodox economics, the G–7's Tokyo communiqué in 1993 clung to the old economic paradigm shared by the BWIs with its slogans: economic growth, deregulation, privatization, productivity, competitiveness, free trade, deficit reduction, investment tax credits, and efficient labor markets. These obsolete slogans map the vanishing textbook territory of 'domestic' economies, now sinking beneath daily trillion-dollar tidal waves of hot currencies in today's global casino. The unwillingness of economists to examine the underlying premises and workings of per capita productivity formulas is a major part of the old paradigm problem. As noted elsewhere, total productivity formulas should include social and environmental productivity, as well as management, capital, investment, research and development, and energy productivity.[16] Social productivity can be statistically highlighted by shifting the focus of national accounts from enterprise production to community production.[17] National accounts must also include both human-built infrastructure and natural resource assets, so that investment in them is distinct from consumption spending. This would allow the derivation of national 'net worth' balance sheets. New Zealand is a leader in developing such asset accounts, which have the added advantage of preventing enterprising politicians from using proceeds from privatization to make their annual budgets appear workable.

Another old paradigm problem concerns the changing nature of money – an extremely useful invention now transmuting from physical indicators to pure information: blips displayed on computer screens or stored on computer disks.[18] National macroeconomic management policies and tools have been rendered less effective by the forces of globalization and vast, international financial flows. Money has become a special form of information, with millions 'made' and 'lost' every second. Today the world's money has shifted from the gold standard to the information standard. Speedy new 'infocurrencies' have short-changed local communities and their capital formation processes everywhere. Local wages deposited in local banks are vacuumed up by interlinked money centers and lost to local businesses, which were already undercut by international merchandizing and production. Small enterprises cannot compete as borrowers at global interest rates.

Today's global casino of massive currency and derivative speculation hedges individual, corporation and bank risks at the expense of increasing systemic risks. It resembles Wall Street in 1929 before the Securities and Exchange Commission (SEC) brought some order to US capital markets. Clearly, a transnational SEC is urgently needed, as well as the tax on currency trading proposed by James Tobin.[19]

Trickle-up vs. Trickle-down Development

Local communities in the global South, as well as in OECD countries, often respond to transnational corporate activity and Bretton Woods projects by organizing credit unions and new forms of micro-lending. They have learned about Bangladesh's Grameen Bank, 'lottery' investment clubs and other grassroots subsistence enterprises in the informal sectors of developing countries (see 'Grameen Bank' in Glossary). Local currencies, such as the Local Exchange Trading Systems (LETS), are proliferating in many OECD countries along with computer-assisted barter clubs, radio 'garage sales', skills exchanges, service credit accounts and direct contracting with local farmers or their markets. The profusion of local initiatives for cutting out expensive intermediaries or global retailing chains are rescuing small merchants and towns, and restoring community cohesion and family values in many OECD countries. Few statistics on these informal sectors exist, because they are cooperative, often 'grant' economies (to use Kenneth Boulding's term). Thus, they remain almost invisible to the BWIs and to national economic statisticians. These functioning traditional, subsistence economies, threatened by global markets, are trying to fight back, but many are rendered invisible by the statistical illusions of GDP.

The BWIs, other global financial institutions and central bankers must recognize that their monopoly on money creation and credit facilities has been broken. Financial TV channels will produce programs such as 'The Venture Capital Show', 'The Private Placement Show' and 'The Initial Public Offering Show' to complement electronic commodity trading screens and securities trading systems, such as Instinet, AutEx and Reuters. Thanks to the recent information technologies, public knowledge and involvement are increasing, making it possible to explore new avenues for revitalizing local economies starved of legal tender by obsolete national policies.

Similarly, policymakers in developing countries are realizing that they no longer need to earn foreign exchange or to yoke their economies to the global casino, but can set up their own computerized exchanges to trade commodities directly on a South–South basis.[20] Such counter-trade and informal 'payments unions' already account for 25 per cent of world trade.[21] The conventional economic paradigm along with the glamour of the World Bank–IMF culture (hotels, limousines and other perks), blind development officials to these methods of bypassing global money cartels. History shows that thousands of US, Canadian and Mexican towns and businesses recovered from the 1930s Great Depression by issuing their own local currencies, scrip, tax-anticipation notes and the like.[22] Ithaca, New York provides a contemporary US example of using local currency. Economists and bankers have often fought these local initiatives despite the fact that they help stabilize sputtering national economies, offer minimal safety nets in case of financial meltdown, and strengthen a successful form of grassroots, trickle-up development.

The same information revolution is also fostering the growth of the global civil society, not only through expensive Internet e-mail systems, but by expanding broadcasting capabilities and linking television facilities to producers. An incipient Global Television Consortium for Sustainable Development will eventually be able to redress TV monoculture with news of grassroots solutions and innovations and fresh multicultural programming. These grassroots TV shows can link small producers in rural areas and developing countries to individual donors, customers and investors who wish to support or buy products directly, via on-screen freephone numbers. Such North–South global home shopping channels can amplify catalogs such as *Oxfam* and *Pueblo to People* and organizations such as Earth Trade, Cultural Survival and Appropriate Technology International. The current paradigm of the BWIs could be supplanted by a trickle-up, informal sector development paradigm that is local, community based, self-reliant, and livelihood-focused. In the twenty-first century, it may not be necessary to leave natural, unspoiled habitats and satisfying communities for job searches in polluted, crime-ridden, urban areas. Every village could have access to opportunity, education, technology and cultural contacts through global, regional and local interactions and information via the new communications 'infostructure'.

Economics and the functioning of the global casino have been exposed as little more than politics in disguise. TV reveals how politics, economics, money, values and cultural traditions interact to direct human affairs, allowing people to understand the implications of the global information society. Even the fruitless debate about how to pay for implementing the sustainable development of *Agenda 21* can be finessed. Most countries' economic policies, when linked with the international financial system, *create* conditions of unsustainability through inappropriate subsidies, improper taxation, faulty macroeconomic management and unsuitable investment and lending policies. Financing sustainable development does not require enormous new sums of money. It requires changing paradigms, priorities and national budgets so that countries stop financing inappropriate programs and policies. As the new paradigm evolves and supporting statistics shift focus, national leaders can more easily re-examine their policies and priorities to remove waste, improper subsidies and counter-productive taxation.

From Economics to Interdisciplinary Systems Policy Models

All economies today are mixed, that is, they are mixtures of markets and regulations, about which orthodox economists have been unable to develop theories. What we call economies are, in reality, sets of rules derived from specific 'cultural DNA codes': the disparate goals and values of different societies. Economists need to defer to cultural anthropologists for an understanding of development patterns of unlike countries.

Table 6.1 Differing Models of Markets and Commons

Economists	*Futurists/Systems*
Markets	*Open Systems*
Private Sector	
Individual Decisions	Divisible Resources
Competition	Win–Lose rules
Invisible hand	(Adam Smith's rules)
Anti-trust	
Commons	*Closed Systems*
Public Sector	
Property of all	Indivisible Resources
Monopoly under Regulation	Win–win rules
Consortia	Cooperation
	Agreements

Note: One must remember that all such schematizations are, at best, approximations and often culturally arbitrary.

The recent awareness of the many faces of capitalism has reintroduced creativity into the sterile thinking and leftover debates from the Cold War.[23] Formula textbooks, demanding US-style economics, have contributed to the suffering in Russia and eastern Europe. In contrast, 'socialism with Chinese characteristics' guides economics in China, whose people seem to understand that markets, like technologies, make good servants but bad masters.[24] A body of academic work supporting market socialism theory has been formulated by, among others, the Chinese Academy of Social Sciences and the State Council's International Technology and Economy Institute's Shanghai branch. Market socialism has much in common with the social markets familiar in G–7 countries, and with the $700 billion socially-responsible investment movement in the United States.

The rush of politicians to adopt free markets and democracy is instinctively correct: complex societies are best governed by feedback from individuals to decision centers. The two key forms of such feedback are *prices* and *votes*. But prices must be corrected to reflect social and environmental costs, and the choices of voters, rather than powerful, special interest groups. These corrections make necessary other forms of feedback, such as indicators and statistics to signal early warning of problems, and independent media to amplify and spotlight issues and concerns. Economic textbooks need to reflect systems theory by teaching how to recognize when markets saturate and turn into commons.[25] (See Table 6.1: Differing Models of Markets and Commons.)

CHANGING INDICATORS

Historical Overview

The interest of social scientists and environmentalists in overhauling the GDP-based System of National Accounts (SNA) emerged at least 40 years ago. By the 1950s, social and natural scientists had started a movement to apply broader indicators in the United States, Canada and Europe for the documentation of social costs. By the 1960s these scientists were critiquing a GDP that, in its simplistic averaging of incomes, could not distinguish between people who were worse off or left out and a few more millionaires. Emile van Lennep, former Secretary General of the OECD, attempted at that time to introduce social indicators into the organization's predominantly economic analyses. Van Lennep encountered objections that such social indicators were normative or value-driven, even though, of course, economic indicators are also normative.[26] Early efforts toward alternative indicators include the work of Richard J. Estes, David Morris, Hazel Henderson, Hirofumi Uzawa, James Tobin and Richard Nordhaus, among others.[27]

New Indicators

Humans measure what they treasure and the emergence of indicators redefining wealth and progress are slowly directing human societies toward sustainability. Pre-eminent is the Human Development Index (HDI) of the UNDP, which ranks 173 countries by a measurement that combines life expectancy, educational attainment and basic purchasing power. The UNDP's public dissemination of annual HDI editions since 1990 has generated unprecedented levels of press attention and controversy. *HDI 1992* brought indicators of the global poverty gap to public attention; *HDI 1993* identified jobless economic growth; and *HDI 1994* with its ranking of countries according to non-economic quality-of-life factors received major television coverage. The indicators have exposed the current hypocrisy of the BWIs,[28] and have opened them logically and morally to demands for the democracy, accountability and restructuring they have prescribed for others. However, the HDI's Human Freedom Index has been criticized by many developing countries as being biased toward Western values. They view the measurement of human rights and other social and environmental indicators as a prelude to the imposition of new conditionalities by the BWIs and Northern bankers, increasing the difficulties of their structural adjustment.

Other important new indicators have received less attention than the high-profile HDI. The World Bank has yet to translate social and environmental indicators such as *SNA 1993* into its operations and projects. The OECD, due partly to van Lennep's early leadership, is producing useful work on environmental indicators.[29] The International Monetary Fund's *World Economic Outlook 1993* received much attention when it issued an April 1993 Addendum that converted conventional per capita GDP rankings to Purchasing Power Parities (PPPs) in order to correct for currency fluctuations and different costs of living. This long-overdue re-ranking by PPPs catapulted China to the position of the world's third largest economy after the United States and Japan. Many private groups produce global indicators and data, notably the on-line services such as Reuters, business publications such as *The Economist*, the World Resources Institute's *World Resources* (five volumes published since 1986), and the Worldwatch Institute's *Vital Signs* and *State of the World* reports.

A milestone *System of National Accounts (SNA 1993)* was published in February 1994. It reflects the official thinking of its sponsoring organizations: the World Bank, IMF, OECD, European Commission, and the UN Statistical Division. This *SNA* offers useful protocols for integrating social and environmental statistics into expanded national accounting frameworks. However, it has many shortcomings that are discussed in greater detail by other contributors to this series. As pointed out by Lourdes Urdaneta-Ferrán,[30] its treatment of labor-force participation, informal sectors, household services and women's work is seriously lacking. The essential role women have always played in human development may now be tracked with the new statistics she has cited. Indeed a paradigm shift is presently occurring at the World Bank, though it has not yet been translated into action: women are finally acknowledged as key actors in development; therefore, an investment in their education would bring high payoffs. Population demographers and policymakers now understand that empowering women is the best contraceptive, and the North South Roundtable's 1993 report, *The United Nations and the Bretton Woods Institutions,*[31] recommends a new UN Agency for the Advancement of Women.

The *System of National Accounts 1993* still emphasizes market-derived data, that along with grossly imperfect pricing, translates into money coefficients that undervalue environmental resources and obscure the full dimensions of 'defensive' costs, that is, those expenditures necessary to mitigate the negative effects of the old paradigm. For example, it is estimated that the growing environmental pollution control industry, now a major employer, will increase from $200 billion in 1990 to $300 billion by the year 2000. Only part of these costs will be subtracted from GDP to arrive at new net indexes. The UN Statistical Division's 1993 *Handbook of National Accounting: Integrated Environmental and Economic Accounting* addresses some of these issues by establishing a statistical alphabet soup that offers, among others, EDP (Environmentally Adjusted Net Domestic Product), ENI (Environmentally Adjusted National Income), SNI (Sustainable National Income) and FISD (Framework of Indicators for Sustainable Development). The UN Statistical Division, the World Bank and many national bureaux of economic analysis agree that numerous social and environmental statistics cannot or should not be aggregated into expanded GNP-type single indexes, such as EDP. Instead, they recommend the new data be offered as satellite accounts, which carry the unfortunate implication that they lack importance. Peter Bartelmus addresses the issues for the UN Statistical Division:

> EDP could be used to define sustainable economic growth in operational terms as: increases in EDP (which allows for the consumption of produced and the depletion and degradation of natural resources), assuming that the allowances made can be invested into capital maintenance and taking into account that past trends of depletion and degradation can be offset or mitigated by technological progress, discovery of natural resources, and changes in consumption patterns.[32]

Even such tortured definitions beg a host of questions about aggregated single indexes such as EDP. How can the public be informed about the assumptions underlying them? How will economists and bureaucrats weight these factors? How will balance-sheet boundaries be drawn between tax-supported programs dealing with stress and illness due to rising unemployment and the corporate downsizing made to bolster productivity and profits? These costs, called 'defensive' expenditures, are averaged into GDP as economic growth, because they create jobs and profits, even though what they are dealing with are the environmental and social disruptions caused by reductions elsewhere. Here, the old paradigm problems concern linear, input–output models of economics and the compartmentalizing of highly interactive economic processes into arbitrary boxes and boundaries. Similarly, GDP double-entry bookkeeping concepts and other macroeconomic categories can no longer clarify what is a 'cost' and what is a 'benefit.' Only interactive systemic models that reflect dynamic changes can manage such new complexities.

The task of overhauling national accounts will be coordinated through the UN, the World Bank, the IMF, the OECD and the European Union. These are the joint promulgators of *SNA 1993*. In April 1994, a year after the Clinton administration ordered the Commerce Department's Bureau of Economic Analysis (BEA) to begin the work of overhauling US national accounts, the first Green GDP was unveiled, but only as an Integrated Economic and Environmental Satellite Account (IEESA).[33] It has many of the problems anticipated by scholars. For example, it uses traditional discount rates that value future consumption as successively less important, thus shortchanging future generations. Also, by treating newly discovered oil and minerals as additions to capital assets, high current consumption levels are made to appear sustainable.[34] In fairness, BEA director, Dr Carol S. Carson, had cautioned earlier against overly high expectations:

> Gross Domestic Product (GDP) – widely used around the world – is a measure of market-oriented economic production. In turn, the level of production largely determines how much a community can consume. While the level of consumption of goods and services, both individually and collectively, is one of the most important factors influencing a community's welfare, there are many others – the existence of peace or war, technology, the environment and income distribution, to name a few. Because these other factors do not enter into the measurement of GDP, additional measures are also needed to evaluate welfare or make policies regarding welfare. It would take a philosopher king to

'add' all the measures relevant to welfare into a single indicator useful for all times and communities; until then, a variety of measures will be needed along with GDP.[35]

Leveling the playing field for statistics, indicators and accounting standards is vital for responsible financial, business and government decision making with a global perspective.

Politics and Indicators

Sustainable development became the rallying cry of some 26,000 representatives of non-governmental organizations (NGOs) at the Rio Earth Summit and Global Forum of 1992. They popularized the demand for new indicators and provided opportunities for coalition building among four major global constituencies:

- environmentalists concerned with green indicators;

- women who push to have household management, parenting, home enterprises and subsistence agriculture accounted for in GDP;[36]

- citizens and NGOs concerned with social justice, urban problems, human rights and corporate and government accountability;

- policymakers in developing countries who are beginning to exploit the bargaining power they have over the North regarding environmental and social issues. This power is based on logic and ethics: why should developing countries have to arrest their own development, when it is Northern industrial countries that have caused the lion's share of pollution and depletion?[37]

In 1989, then-President Carlos Andres Perez of Venezuela challenged the economistic focus of IMF structural adjustment conditionalities by gathering statistics about their adverse effects on social programs, children and the environment.[38] At the Earth Summit, Southern NGOs estimated the Northern hemisphere's pollution debt to the world at $15–20 trillion. This was put on the negotiating table at the Global Forum, to balance the discussion of the South's debt to Northern banks and governments, and the issues of clean-up costs and transference of green technologies.

119

Military Spending and Human Development Performance

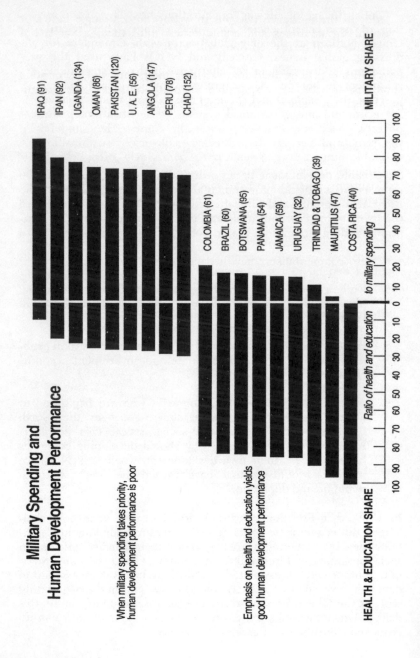

When military spending takes priority,
human development performance is poor

Emphasis on health and education yields
good human development performance

IRAQ (91)
IRAN (92)
UGANDA (134)
OMAN (86)
PAKISTAN (120)
U. A. E. (56)
ANGOLA (147)
PERU (78)
CHAD (152)

COLOMBIA (61)
BRAZIL (60)
BOTSWANA (95)
PANAMA (54)
JAMAICA (59)
URUGUAY (32)
TRINIDAD & TOBAGO (39)
MAURITIUS (47)
COSTA RICA (40)

MILITARY SHARE

to military spending

Ratio of health and education

HEALTH & EDUCATION SHARE

100 90 80 70 60 50 40 30 20 10 0 10 20 30 40 50 60 70 80 90 100

Global linkage of citizens' organizations has allowed the formation of new constituencies for world change. They regard the United Nations as the only global actor with a mandate for addressing global issues. Citizens and NGOs have used the new paradigms and criteria to set alternative paths to sustainable development in motion. These groups know it is not enough to describe the *symptoms* and *effects* of the existing unsustainable global economic and geopolitical systems (desertification, pollution, poverty, injustice), they emphasize the *causes*. They understand the structural barriers to achieving ecologically sustainable and equitable human development, and, increasingly, offer socially innovative solutions.[39]

Coalitions, such as the '50 Years is Enough' campaign, detail an inequitable global economic order, reinforced by the outdated workings of the BWIs, and the General Agreement on Tariffs and Trade (GATT). They point to grossly unequal terms of trade, Northern dominance over the UN, and a global arms race that still accounts for about a trillion dollars annually. *HDI 1994* documents a decline in the arms trade on average of 3 per cent per year since 1987. This has yielded a 'peace dividend', which has somehow become statistically invisible in most countries. The United States, Russia, the United Kingdom, France and Germany – are still selling weapons to every dictator and warlord around the world. This emphasizes the usefulness of the HDI's ratio indicators of military to civilian expenditures (see Figure 6.2: Military Spending and Human Development Performance), and the groundbreaking work of Ruth Leger Sivard and her Washington-based World Military and Social Expenditures.[40]

New levels of subtlety have been reached, making the questioning of the values underlying economic systems unavoidable. GDP indicators of progress and measures of wealth naturally become targets of grassroots activists and other constituencies for change. These indicators were promulgated in government agencies behind closed doors, and their formulas for weighting incommensurable statistics were arrived at through the use of arcane economic computer models that are maddeningly inaccessible to activists. Even when challenged by public interest advocates in the scientific community, economists in these status quo bureaucracies claim that only those

---

Opposite.
Figure 6.2 Military Spending and Human Development Performance
(Adapted from The Human Development Report 1991, *UNDP, New York)*

with Ph.D.s in economics can possibly understand the 'scientific' construction of their indexes. Traditional academic etiquette discourages many experts from other disciplines from invading the economists' turf, and even motivated social and environmental scientists often lack the time, courage or resources to perform the necessary critical analyses.

The HDI program at the UNDP encountered considerable hostility from economists, even those of the UN's statistical offices who were the architects of the GDP-based UN System of National Accounts (UNSNA). Defensiveness and a 'not invented here' reaction emerged as HDI indicators revealed long-term patterns, such as widening poverty gaps and jobless economic growth, that had been glossed over by the per capita averaged UNSNA. HDI will become more politicized as it is refined into an ever-sharper tool, capable of holding governments accountable for their progress toward sustainable human development.

Professional economists still decree that the World Bank's focus will remain on the concerns of lenders and capital markets.[41] The Bank's *World Development Report 1994* broke new ground by focusing on the huge sustainable development payoffs from investments in health and education. But on the whole, for reasons inherent in the Bank's structure,[42] it is still heavily oriented toward neoclassical economic views similar to those of Lawrence Summers (previously the World Bank's Chief Economist and then Treasury Department Under-Secretary for International Affairs in the Clinton administration).[43] However, the desire of traditional GDP economists to cling to old data and formulas for the sake of historic comparability can be overcome by introducing the new national and satellite accounts in parallel with GDP for as long as necessary.

Inertia and fierce resistance from other powerful quarters toward reformulating GDP continue to slow the shift to sustainability. GDP indexes have become a bulwark underlying the Western industrial way of life, sustaining power centers in business and government. The SNA also has powerful vested interests in academia: shifts to new indicators would require complete revamping of economic textbooks, courses, and prestigious business and management programs in universities everywhere. There are tens of thousands of tenured Ph.D. economists on powerful faculty committees and journal editorial boards who have a vested interest in the status quo.[44]

The development and use of accurate indicators of sustainable development demand that the broader indicators be interdisciplinary. Economists who have heretofore resisted interference in their demolation of macroeconomic policy now make use of a few social scientists and environmentalists, though they usually insist on retaining control of policy models and frameworks. Furthermore, they have vastly superior access to the funds that maintain this control. However, gauging the progress of complex multidimensional societies by using the approach of a single discipline, is, on the face of it, absurd.[45] (See Figure 6.3: The World's Women: Working Hours.)

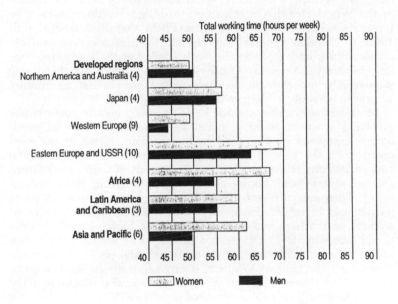

Women in most regions spend as much or more time working than men when unpaid housework is taken into account.
Note: Numbers in parenthesis refer to the number of studies in each region.

Figure 6.3
The World's Women: Working Hours – Trends and Statistics
(Source: The World's Women 1970–1990, United Nations, New York)

Unbundling the Aggregated Indexes

The unbundled indexes of major quality-of-life aspects (including economic data) present an overview that allows voters to weight the indicators by focusing on what most concerns them. Jacksonville, Florida takes this approach, often using as many as 80 to 100 indicators that are recalibrated annually through citizen input. The Sustainable Seattle Indicators construct data with input from voters, who are also involved in regular reviews of the civic progress toward the targeted goals. The London-based New Economics Foundation has launched a similar project in British cities in cooperation with local United Nations Associations. At all levels of society, there is a drive, spearheaded by Dr Ilona Kickbusch of the World Health Organization, to design healthier cities. The International Association of Architects held a world competition in 1993 to develop criteria and models for designing sustainable communities, and a movement with similar goals is growing rapidly in North America. Quality-of-life indicators are becoming increasingly important to the business and investment community as predictive tools for longer-term asset evaluation.

Most business and economic journals now regularly cover issues involving green accounting, taxation, life-cycle analyses of products – signposts on the road to internalizing formerly excluded costs. With the goal of correcting prices to reflect environmental and social constraints and realities, thousands of corporate balance sheets, reports and books are now incorporating these indicators.[46] They measure real things, for example, parts per million of particulates in urban air, literacy rates, infant mortality, ratios of soldiers to teachers and poverty gaps. One Dutch-based multinational company, BSO Origin, has produced an annual report with state-of-the-art accounting of its environmental performance since 1990. Its CEO, Eckart Wintzen, is crusading to change European value-added taxes (VAT) to a more ecologically and actuarially correct levy he terms value-*extracted* taxes (VET).

The main weakness of HDI is that it still employs economic methods to aggregate diverse elements, usually using traditional weighting to come up with a ready-made, eye- and media-catching analog of GDP. Herman Daly acknowledges this problem with his Index of Sustainable Economic Welfare (ISEW).[47] The trade-off is that a single-number index will gain media coverage at the cost of misinterpretation – the arcane assumptions behind it are impossible to sort out. Some economists concerned with sustainable development feel that societies should not employ overall indexes, which are misleading.[48]

Making Indicators Democratic: the Politics of Meaning

Democratic indicators of human progress and sustainable development foster a politics of meaning based on a broader, longer-term bottom line that measures results so politicians can be held accountable. Editors and reporters need to be made aware of the debate over sustainable paths to development,[49] then the media can spread the concepts – if they can conquer their fear of losing advertisers and their addiction to single indexes amenable to sound-bites. Creative media producers are needed to design news and documentary formats for radio and television. For example, a 'Country Scorecards' program is needed to cover quality-of-life indicators, domestically and between nations, on a regular basis. The time is ripe since indicators such as those of the daily newspaper, *USA Today*, the witty diverse juxtapositions in *Harpers*, and the expanded coverage in other popular magazines are becoming a fad.

To address the problem of over-aggregation and mystification, the Country Futures Indicators (CFI)[50] are unbundled to be transparent, multidisciplinary and accessible to the public. CFI includes the major categories and subcategories deemed necessary to form a generic, comparable model. Any city, province or country can delve into the CFI to extract and develop its own indicators according to its needs, values and goals. Truly sustainable development will require, at the least, the inclusion of all CFI categories; an interdisciplinary group of statisticians to develop measurements; and unbundled indicators, with the data separated and released to the public and media, rather than obscured by aggregation.[51] The formulation of these sustainable development indicators requires top-notch research to survey and collate the wealth of available data. A March 1993 opinion survey on democratic reforms found that 73 per cent of Americans favor such additional indicators to complement GDP.[52] A follow-up survey in April 1994, which included the same question on quality-of-life indicators, plus two opposing arguments, garnered 78 per cent approval.

The fears of many policymakers in Southern governments, as mentioned earlier, are understandable, because HDI and green indicators are normative in the sense that they focus on what that society considers important. Many see sustainable development indicators as a Northern plot to make access to loans more difficult, or to force their cultures to conform to Western values. However, the statistical demands of developing countries must be multidisciplinary because each country has its own cultural DNA code around which specific indicators must be designed.[53] Therefore, formulating them will diverge methodologically from traditional national accounting, which uses only economic coefficients and weighting formulas. GDP is normative, non-transparent, and unaccountable to electorates, as opposed to sustainable development indicators that can be tailored to the individual country.

Economists are not sitting by idly as their turf is invaded by other statisticians and corporate reformers such as the Business Council on Sustainable Development, which published its manifesto, *Changing Course*, in 1992.[54] They are becoming professionally entrepreneurial. Some have put new labels on the old wine bottles; others are reformatting résumés and business cards, calling themselves ecological economists, natural-resource economists, or environmental economists to catch the lucrative new green markets. They often take speciously quantitative, pseudo-rigorous approaches to specific environmental indicators.[55] The main intellectual problem with ecological economics is the general assumption that if a natural resource has a value between zero and infinity, then an ecological economist can calculate its contingent price by using 'willingness to pay' or 'willingness to be compensated' formulas. For example, to arrive at the monetary value of a marshland (one of the most productive ecosystems on the planet), economists poll voters and residents with no profit motive and little knowledge other than deep appreciation and a desire to preserve it. The contingent prices arrived at in this way would surely be lower than those offered by a hotel developer with a profit motive, or by a biotechnology firm that had identified species in the area it could use for pharmaceutical products.

This fancy new math is hiding neoclassical assumptions such as the Pareto principle, which ignores issues such as the informal economy, job losses, and disparities in wealth, income, power and information among people and countries. Such flawed pricing, especially for essentials, discounts poor peoples' needs and concerns because they cannot afford to pay or participate. This is not to say that environmental resources should be treated as 'free' or priced at zero, as they are in GDP, but to caution against a narrow, money-driven evaluation method. Economists believe deeply in money coefficients and prices, however imperfectly derived from flawed or even fictitious markets. But the pricing system for ecosystems should be subordinated to democratic decision making, that is, voting on whether to protect the marsh. Similar concerns challenge economists who advocate the pricing and trading of licenses to pollute, instigated in 1991 in the United States by the Chicago Board of Trade. Amazingly, companies are able to trade such pollution licenses without consulting citizens living in the surrounding areas.

Economists have little training in understanding social systems or the productive functions of ecosystems. They are pitted against those concerned with human, environmental and aesthetic values in estimating the worth of natural resources. Their economic approach should, at the least, jettison neoclassical welfare and market formulas and price such priceless resources as biodiversity or rain-forests at the cost of replacement. Most social and natural scientists, as well as voters in the United States, believe that economists must begin to work within interdisciplinary teams that include statisticians from health, education, environment and other social policy fields. New national accounting methods designed to correct GDP fallacies will function like spliced-in cultural DNA strands bringing sounder, healthier development patterns to human societies. *Quantitative* growth is dominant in children, but once mature size and weight are reached, *qualitative* growth becomes central – education, social skills, broad awareness, even greater ethical understanding and wisdom. The shift in society from GDP statistics to sustainable indicators mirrors the maturing of individuals. It illuminates the human traits that must be developed if societies are to be restructured for sustainability.

Ecological economists need to forge methodological links with holistic social approaches, like those of the HDI team, the Society for the Advancement of Social Economics and Canada's Green Indicators. Many advocate green taxes, which have the advantage of correcting prices to reflect costs of production that were formerly excluded from company balance sheets. This would have the ultimate effect of redirecting corporate enterprises.[56] The United Nations could collect these global green taxes on various forms of pollution to fund grassroots sustainable development.

Narrow views of environmental and natural resources can shortchange other needed corrections of GDP such as the inclusion of unpaid work and acknowledgement of poverty gaps. Some of these corrections may further alienate the South, where there is not yet much long-term thinking on environmental preservation. As they see it, poverty is the greatest pollution problem. These reactions and the South's possible opposition to new indicators are justified, and they could jeopardize the movement to adopt them. So, despite a body of important work on valuing resources and energy consumption,[57] poverty issues must be included as an aspect of sustainable development indicators.

Indicators of sustainability will evolve, yet retain country specific dimensions. Textbook formulas for economic growth fail because there are no 'correct' rates of savings, investments or exports. Some economists understand the need to broaden their analyses from equilibrium-based macroeconomic models to systems and chaos theory, in order to capture accelerating rates of change. (See Table 6.2: Emerging Change Models.) Academic courses on sustainable development should include statistical source material, evaluation of data reliability, reviews of major efforts in the field, and critiques of different approaches and development paradigms. It remains for economists to relinquish their neocolonization of national policy via GDP and other macroeconomic statistics and collaborate with world-wide interdisciplinary efforts to promote indicators that can help all countries reach sustainable development.

Table 6.2 Emerging Change Models

Earth System Science	Interdisciplinary: plate tectonics, biogeochemical and solar-driven process, strato and meso-sphere (NASA Program on Global Change International Division, Washington DC 20546)
Catastrophe Mathematics	Models at least seven modes in which systems change their states, i.e. bifurcations (Rene Thom, *Structural Stability and Morphogenesis*, Paris, 1972)
Cybernetic Models	Homeostasis and metamorphosis governed by feedbacks, negative and positive (Magoroh Maruyama, 'Paradigmatology', in H. Henderson, *Politics of the Solar Age*, 1981)
Order through fluctuation Models	(Ilya Prigogine, *From Being to Becoming*, San Francisco, 1980)
Chaos Theory Based on Attractors	Point, periodic and chaotic attractors can 'magnetize' systems into new states (Ralph Abraham, *Dynamics: The Geometry of Behavior*, Santa Cruz, 1984)

RECOMMENDATIONS AND CONCLUSION

For nearly 50 Cold War years, the superpowers and their blocs competed militarily. In today's uneasy interregnum, religious, cultural and ethical conflicts have resurfaced, along with competing trade blocs that have created global competition tantamount to economic warfare. Another post-Cold War dilemma is how to manage our densely populated societies and cities on a small, polluted planet. The human family will soon have six billion members. We are consuming and competing for resources at an unprecedented rate. Millions of refugees are forced to flee collapsing ecosystems and the societies once supported by them.

Beyond the collapse of communism, the Bretton Woods institutions must face the task of reshaping nineteenth-century textbook capitalism to meet the challenges of interdependence and sustainable forms of human development. It seems clear that the World Bank should relinquish management of the Global Environment Facility. Even though it is co-managed with the UN Environment Program and UNDP, its lending is directed by old economic paradigms and will continue to destroy local communities by forcing millions to relocate in the path of its ill-conceived projects.

The World Trade Organization (WTO) could, with scorecards that enable trade pacts to include new criteria and measure progress on major goals, help elevate and level the global playing field. Global ethical consciousness can be raised so that the best managed and most responsible companies and countries can prosper in a win–win world. Definitions of human security and well-being emerging from member countries and UN agencies include the right to development (made possible by access to credit), along with health, education and human rights.

At its 50th anniversary, the United Nations can be strengthened to meet new challenges and become a vital provider of valuable services. There are no good arguments for preventing the United Nations from floating its own bonds, once arrears are paid up and dues made mandatory. As the United Nations is given taxation authority over international arms sales and currency trading, such bonds would become more saleable. However, a $700 billion market for UN bonds probably exists today composed of future-oriented, socially responsible, globally concerned and patient investors. The high-level meeting convened in February 1993 by the US-based Ford Foundation to consider whether the United Nations should issue bonds was co-chaired by Paul Volcker, former chairman of the US Federal Reserve Board, and

Karl Otto Pohl, former president of Germany's Bundesbank, with a full array of conservative financiers in attendance. Predictably and with a profound lack of vision, these custodians of the status quo agreed that the United Nations should not be allowed to issue bonds. A more innovative group of financiers, including those from socially responsible investment sectors, should be convened to consider not only how to restructure the Bretton Woods institutions, but the whole range of UN funding proposals, so it can fulfill its new role.

Table 6.3 The Emerging Global Playing Field

New markets	*New commons*
Telecom services	Space, Earth systems science
Desert greening	Electromagnetic spectrum
Pollution control	Oceans, water resources
Renewable energy	Atmosphere, ozone layer
Recycling, eco-resource management	Security, peacekeeping
'Caring' sector (day care, counselling, re-hab, nursing)	Forests
Infrastructure (extending transport, telecommunications, etc.)	Health
Eco-restoration, bio-remediation	Global economy

Lastly, the United Nations could set up a new public–private agency, the United Nations Security Insurance Agency (UNSIA) modeled on INTELSAT in the communications field[58] and the World Bank in the development field. UNSIA could provide a substantial source of revenue for peacekeeping and peacemaking while giving member states more security for less money.[59] Initial calculations suggest that UNSIA would eventually provide giant markets for insurance companies, allowing defense budgets to be cut by as much as 50 per cent. These funds could be redirected toward investments in health and education, recognized at last by economists to be keys to development. Countries buying such insurance would be able to lower their rates by reducing their military forces and putting more of them at the disposal of UN peacekeeping and conflict prevention task forces.

In sum, the new paradigm of development calls for new criteria and indicators, as well as a creative response by communities and global institutions, most notably the United Nations. (See Table 6.3: The Emerging Global Playing Field.)

Notes

1. World Commission on Environment and Development, *Our Common Future* (Oxford and New York: Oxford University Press, 1987). Also known as the 'Brundtland Report' after commission chair Gro Harlem Brundtland.
2. Office of the Secretary General, United Nations, New York, NY. Released May 25, 1994.
3. United Nations, *Agenda 21, UNCED Concluding Document: Press Summary* (New York: United Nations Department of Public Information, 1992).
4. For example, see Hazel Henderson, *Politics of the Solar Age: Alternatives to Economics* (Garden City, NY: Anchor Press/Doubleday, 1981), chapter 8: 'Three Hundred Years of Snake Oil'.
5. Rachel Carson, *Silent Spring* (Boston: Houghton Mifflin, 1992).
6. United Nations, *Agenda 21, UNCED Concluding Document: Press Summary*. Also see Daniel Sitarz (ed.), *Agenda 21: The Earth Summit Strategy to Save Our Planet* (Boulder, CO: EarthPress, 1993).
7. Hazel Henderson, *Paradigms In Progress* (Indianapolis, IN: Knowledge Systems, 1991), chapter 6.
8. Henderson, *Paradigms in Progress*.
9. David Felix, 'The Tobin Tax Proposal: Background, Issues and Prospects', *Futures*, vol. 27/2, (March 1995) pp. 195–208.
10. 'No Need for a Boost' in *The Economist* (February 13, 1993), pp. 15–16.
11. 'Workers of the World, Compete' in *The Economist*, April 2, 1994, pp. 69–70.
12. Paul Wallich, 'Lies, Damned Lies and Models' in *Scientific American*, January 1994, p. 151.
13. Small and family businesses in the United States still produce over half of all goods and services and provide millions of jobs; and family businesses in western Europe account for almost two-thirds of its employment and GDP, somewhat compensating for the downsizing and moving offshore of large companies.
14. 'Don't Blame the Slow Job Growth on Labor Costs' in *Business Week* (July 12, 1993), p. 120.
15. 'Don't Blame the Slow Job Growth on Labor Costs'.
16. Henderson, *Politics of the Solar Age*, chapter 9.

17. See Sixto Roxas, chapter 1 of this volume.
18. Joel Kurtzman, *The Death of Money: How the Electronic Economy has Destabilized the World's Markets and Created Financial Chaos* (New York: Simon and Schuster, 1993).
19. United Nations Development Programme, *Human Development Report 1994* (New York: Oxford University Press, 1995), p. 90. For currency proposals, see Bernard Lietaer and Jane D'Arista, appendices to *Rethinking Bretton Woods: Conference Report and Recommendations*, available separately from the Center of Concern, Washington, DC. For discussion of the Tobin tax proposal, see Stephany Griffith-Jones and Vassilis Papageorgiou, 'Globalization of Financial Markets and Impact on Flows to LDCs: New Challenges for Regulation' in Jo Marie Griesgraber and Bernhard G. Gunter (eds), *Rethinking Bretton Woods*, Vol. 4, *The World's Monetary System: Towards Stability and Sustainability in the Twenty-first Century*, (London: Pluto Press with the Center of Concern, forthcoming).
20. South Commission, *The Challenge to the South: Report of the South Commission* (London and New York: Oxford University Press, 1990).
21. Bart S. Fisher, 'Introduction' in Bart S. Fisher and Kathleen M. Harte (eds), *Barter in the World Economy* (New York: Praeger, 1985), p. 1, referring to a study by the US International Trade Commission (USITC), *Analysis of Recent Trends in U.S. Countertrade*, prepared principally by Ronald J. DeMarines (Washington, DC: USITC, 1982).
22. Earlier examples include the city of Worgl in Austria and the Channel Islands of Jersey and Guernsey off the south coast of Britain. All three became enclaves of prosperity and survived botched national policies of the period. For example, see Ralph A. Mitchell and Neil Shafer, *Standard Catalog of Depression Scrip of the United States in the 1930s: Including Canada and Mexico* (Iola, WI: Krause Publications, 1985).
23. For example, see Charles Hampden-Turner and Fons Trompenaar, *The Seven Cultures of Capitalism* (New York: Doubleday, 1993).
24. For example, see William H. Overholt, *The Rise of China* (New York: Norton, 1993).
25. Henderson, *Paradigms In Progress*, chapter 7: 'Greening the Economy and Recycling Economics'.
26. Conversation with the author, London, April 1991.
27. Henderson, *Politics of the Solar Age*, chapter 13; Richard J. Estes, *Trends in World Social Development: The Social Progress of Nations, 1970–1987* (New York: Praeger, 1988). Early examples of alternative indicators are the 'Index of Social Progress' (ISP) devised by Richard J. Estes in 1974, and the 'Physical Quality of Life Index' (PQLI) developed by David Morris for the Overseas Development Council of Washington, DC.

The author was also involved in the efforts in the 1970s toward alternative indicators. As a member of President Carter's Economic Task Force for his election campaign in 1975, I recommended expanding the President's Council of Economic Advisors into an interdisciplinary Council of Social Science Advisors, and expanding the Federal Reserve Board of Governors to include representatives of consumers, employees and environmentalists. In 1973, my research in Japan examined efforts at deducting environmental costs from GNP. Hirofumi Uzawa had written a paper on the need for adding a capital consumption account to GNP to measure depletion of national resources. See Hirofumi Uzawa as cited in Hazel Henderson, *Creating Alternative Futures: The End of Economics* (New York: Berkeley Publishing Corporation, 1978), p. 52.

Other early efforts by economists are summarized in Henderson, *Paradigms In Progress*, chapter 6.

28. See Katarina Tomasevski, 'Human Rights Impact Assessment: Proposals for the Next 50 Years of Bretton Woods' in Jo Marie Griesgraber and Bernhard G. Gunter (eds), *Rethinking Bretton Woods*, Vol. 1, *Promoting Development: Effective Global Institutions for the Twenty-first Century* (London: Pluto Press with the Center of Concern, 1995), chapter 4.

29. A working paper by John C. O'Connor provides a recent overview of current work at the Bank, the OECD and other agencies: John C. O'Connor, 'Towards Environmentally Sustainable Development: Measuring Progress' from the International Union for Conservation of Nature and Natural Resources–World Conservation Union, 19th Session, General Assembly (Buenos Aires, Argentina, January 1994).

30. Lourdes Urdaneta-Ferrán, 'Rethinking Statistical Requirements: Gender Statistics and Accounts' in Jo Marie Griesgraber and Bernhard G. Gunter (eds), *Rethinking Bretton Woods*, Vol. 1, *Promoting Development: Effective Global Institutions for the Twenty-first Century* (London: Pluto Press with the Center of Concern, 1995), chapter 5.

31. North South Roundtable, Society for International Development, *The United Nations and the Bretton Woods Institutions: New Challenges for the 21st Century* (New York: North South Roundtable, Society for International Development, 1993).

32. United Nations Statistical Division, *Handbook of National Accounting: Integrated Environmental and Economic Accounting* (New York: United Nations, 1993).

33. US Department of Commerce, 'Integrated Economic and Environmental Satellite Accounts' in *Survey of Current Business*, vol. 74, no. 4 (April 1994) pp. 33–49.

34. US Department of Commerce, 'Integrated Economic and Economic Satellite Accounts', p. 39.

35. Interview with the author.
36. See Henderson, *Paradigms In Progress*, chapters 4 and 6; and Marilyn Waring, *If Women Counted* (San Francisco: Harpers, 1988).
37. Statistics abound on the vast asymmetry between North and South in relative emission of pollutants, energy consumption, etc., which indicate that industrial countries owe a large share for the clean-up costs and must reduce their own wasteful consumption.
38. Waring, *If Women Counted*.
39. Hazel Henderson, 'Social Innovation and Citizen Movements' in *Futures*, vol. 25, no. 3 (April 1993), pp. 322–38.
40. Ruth Leger Sivard, *World Military and Social Expenditures*, 14th edition (Washington, DC: World Priorities, Inc., 1991).
41. Progress is slow, in spite of yeoman work by Herman Daly (now at the University of Maryland), Robert Goodland, Ernst Lutz, Mohamed el Ashry, and others in the environmental department, as well as Ismail Serageldin, vice president for Sustainable Development, who understands the new issues well.
42. See Moises Naim, 'The World Bank: Its Role, Governance and Organizational Culture' in *Bretton Woods: Looking to the Future* (Washington, DC: Bretton Woods Commission, July 1994) pp. C–273–287.
43. Summers' now infamous internal memo about *encouraging* dirty industries to relocate in poor countries illustrates the conceptual problems that neoclassical economists have in coming to grips with broader concepts such as sustainable development. 'Let Them Eat Pollution' in *The Economist*, February 8, 1992, p. 66.
44. Such academic sniping was witnessed during the confirmation of the Chair of President Clinton's Council of Economic Advisors, Laura D'Andrea Tyson – a fairly conventional structural economist and hardly a sustainable development innovator.
45. Sustainable development indicators require the input of economists and statisticians from many disciplines. For example, from the World Health Organization (WHO) in health care, from UNESCO in education and literacy, from UN Population and Family Planning in gender-specific indicators (see Figure 6.3: The World's Women: Working Hours), from the ILO in work-place issues, from International Consumers Union in consumer/environmental impact statistics, and from UNEP in environment. Another example is Nancy Rodriguez, MD, President of Venezuela's Institute for Advanced Study (IDEA) in Caracas who favors broad indicators, with additional measures of child development. She is helping upgrade Venezuela's national accounts. See Nancy Rodriguez, 'Redefining Wealth and Progress' in *The Caracas Report on Alternative Development Indicators* (Indianapolis, IN: Knowledge Systems, 1990). Other

multidisciplinary approaches include such successful indicators as Jacksonville, Florida's Quality Indicators of Progress, operating since 1983.

46. The municipal bond rating firms, Moody's and Standard and Poor's, use quality-of-life indicators in rating municipal bonds. The Calvert Group, Inc., managers of over $1 billion in socially responsible mutual funds, is currently collaborating with this author on a version of 'Country Future Indicators' (CFI) for quality-of-life measurement in the United States. *Fortune* magazine recently published a green scorecard, citing the ten best and ten worst companies, with data compiled from the respected non-profit, public-interest research group, the Council on Economic Priorities of New York. A spate of new volumes on green accounting have appeared, such as *Green Reporting*, edited by Dave Owen (London, New York: Chapman and Hall, University and Professional Division, 1992) and *Coming Clean: Corporate Environmental Reporting*, by Deloitte Touche Tohmatsu International and the International Institute of Sustainable Development, London (London: Touche Ross and Co., 1993).

47. Herman E. Daly and John B. Cobb, Jr, *For the Common Good: Redirecting the Economy Towards Community, the Environment and a Sustainable Future* (Boston: Beacon Press, 1989).

48. Ismail Serageldin advocates a balance between economic, social, and environmental indicators.

49. Videotape of C-Span national coverage of Hazel Henderson press briefing on 'Redefining Wealth and Progress' at the National Press Club, Washington, DC, May 1993, co-sponsored by the University of Missouri School of Journalism's New Directions for News. (Available from Public Affairs Archives, Purdue University, 1000 Liberal Arts and Education Building, West Lafayette, Indiana 47907–1000.) I was encouraged by the size of the group of media attendees and their thoughtful questions and comments.

50. Calvert Group and Hazel Henderson, *The Calvert–Henderson Quality-of-Life Indicators for the United States* (Bethesda, MD: Calvert Group, Inc., forthcoming, Fall 1995).

51. This is the approach of the first version of CFI, *The Calvert–Henderson Quality-of-Life Indicators for the United States*, to be published as a public education service of the Calvert Group, Inc., in Fall 1995, with a planned media syndication thereafter.

52. Americans Talk Issues Foundation, *Survey #22: On Improving Democracy in America* (St. Augustine, FL: Americans Talk Issues Foundation, 1993).

53. The South Commission took this approach in its report, *The Challenge to the South*.

54. Stephan Schmidheiny, *Changing Course: A Global Business Perspec-*

tive on Development and the Environment (Cambridge, MA: Massachusetts Institute of Technology Press, 1992).

55. Macroeconomists who are still trying to expand GDP into welfare indexes by pricing environmental amenities and costs include the United Kingdom's David Pearce and Partha Dasgupta and in the United States, Robert Solow and Herman Daly, the designer with John and Clifford Cobb, of ISEW. The International Institute for Ecological Economics uses similar as well as broader interdisciplinary approaches, as found in their journal, *Ecological Economics* (Amsterdam, New York: Elsevier Press), published since 1989, and in 1991 volume of the same title, edited by Robert Costanza of the University of Maryland. Frances Cairncross uses this approach in her 1991 *Costing the Earth* (Cambridge: Harvard Business School Press, 1992) and her columns in *The Economist*.

56. Ernst Ulrich von Weizsäcker's *Ecological Tax Reform* (London: Zed Books, 1992) is a reference source on green taxes, and his Wuppertal Institute is doing groundbreaking work on ecological taxation.

57. For example, the World Resources Institute's Robert Repetto in valuing forest resources in Indonesia and Costa Rica; Robert Costanza's work on the value of wetlands (based on Howard T. Odum's net energy analyses at the University of Florida); and case studies by Ernst Lutz, Salah El Serafy, John Pezzey, Joachim von Amsberg and others at the World Bank.

58. For more on INTELSAT, see Marcellus S. Snow, *The International Telecommunications Satellite Organization, INTELSAT: Economic and Institutional Challenges Facing an International Organization* (Huntsville, AL: International Book Import Service, Inc., 1987).

59. Alan F. Kay and Hazel Henderson 'Policy Document: United Nations Security Insurance Agency (UNSIA)', Participant Paper 2A for Roundtable on Global Change, July 22–24, 1994 (St. Augustine, FL: Center for Sustainable Development and Alternative World Futures, 1994).

Glossary

African Development Bank (AfDB) – An international development finance institution owned by 76 member governments, including 51 regional members from Africa and 25 non-regional, mostly industrialized nations. The Bank, which is headquartered in Abidjan, Côte d'Ivoire, was founded as a purely African self-help initiative in 1963 and began with only US$250 million in capital, none of which came from the world's industrialized nations. In 1982, the AfDB accepted developed countries as members.

Agenda 21 – The main strategy document for environmentally responsible development for the next century from the United Nations Conference on Environment and Development (UNCED) in Rio de Janeiro, June 1992. *Agenda 21* is an action plan covering over 100 program areas and includes commitments of international aid to protect natural habitats and biodiversity and to alleviate poverty.

American Economic Cooperation Administration – The American counterpart to the Organization for European Economic Cooperation designed to implement the European Recovery Programme, which grew out of Marshall Aid provided by the United States and Canada to the western European countries for recovery after World War II.

Asian Development Bank (ADB) – An international development finance institution owned by 52 member governments, including 19 industrialized nations in Europe, North America, Asia and the Pacific, and 33 developing nations. The Bank, which is headquartered in Manila, was created in 1966 on recommendation of the United Nations Economic Commission for Asia and the Far East to accelerate economic development in the developing countries of Asia.

Beggar-thy-neighbor policies – Economic policies by one country to improve its domestic economy, but which have adverse effects on other economies, such as competitive devaluations and tariffs.

Balance-of-payments deficit/surplus – A country is said to have a balance-of-payments deficit when its income (credits from exports, cash inflows, loans, etc.) is less than its payments (debits from imports, cash outflows, debt repayments, etc.). A balance-of-payments surplus occurs when income is greater than payments.

Bank for International Settlement (BIS) – An intergovernmental financial institution originally established in 1930 to assist and coordinate the transfer of payments among national central banks. This contrasts with the Board of Governors of the IMF which is comprised of Ministers of Finance. The creation of the IMF constrained the subsequent expansion of the BIS's international monetary role and activities. Main current activities of the bank are to assist central banks in managing and investing their monetary reserves, and to collect and disseminate information on macroeconomic topics and international monetary affairs.

Bretton Woods institutions (BWIs) – The institutions founded at the conference of Bretton Woods, New Hampshire, in 1944, that is, the World Bank and the International Monetary Fund (IMF).

Committee of Twenty (C–20) – Established by the IMF's Board of Governors in light of the events following August 15, 1971, when President Nixon suspended the convertibility of US dollars into gold. The committee consisted of one member appointed by each country or group of countries which appoints or elects an executive director of the Fund. The Committee decided to let a new monetary system evolve gradually out of existing arrangements and completed its work in 1974.

Debt crisis – Extreme difficulties of many developing countries to repay their loans since 1982, caused mainly by drastically increasing interest rates in the hard currency creditor countries and a slowing world economy which led to lower exports.

Debt write-down – An internal decision of a bank to reassess the value of an outstanding loan and adjust its internal accounts to reflect reduced expectation of full repayment. The debt is written-down in the bank's books, but the debtor country is not forgiven its debt or required to repay less.

Deflation – The opposite of inflation, that is, a sustained fall in the general price level.

Depreciation/devaluation – A decrease in the value of a currency. If the exchange rate is defined in terms of foreign currency over domestic currency, then a devaluation of the domestic currency implies a decrease of the exchange rate. If the exchange rate is defined in terms of domestic currency over foreign currency, then a devaluation of the domestic currency implies an increase of the exchange rate.

Development (equitable, sustainable and participatory) – A healthy growing economy which (a) distributes the benefits widely, (b) meets the needs of the present generation without compromising the needs of future generations, and (c) provides for human rights and freedoms, effective governance, and increasing democratization.

Development Committee – Officially the 'Joint Ministerial Committee of the Boards of Governors of the World Bank and the IMF on the Transfer of Real Resources to Developing Countries'. Established in October 1974, it currently consists of 24 members, generally Ministers of Finance, appointed in turn to successive periods of two years by one of the countries or groups of countries that designates a member of the World Bank's or the IMF's Board of Executive Directors. The Committee advises and reports to the Boards of Governors of the World Bank and the IMF.

Economic and Social Council (ECOSOC) – One of the original six major organs of the United Nations. It coordinates the economic and social work of the UN and the specialized agencies and institutions. The council makes recommendations and initiatives relating to all economic and social questions.

Enhanced Structural Adjustment Facility (ESAF) – Introduced in 1988, ESAF is disbursed by the IMF as a trustee. Objectives, eligibility, terms and basic program features of ESAF parallel those of the Structural Adjustment Facility (SAF). However, the adjustment measures are much stronger than for SAF and a detailed policy framework paper is prepared each year.

European Recovery Programme – Following a proposal for US assistance to Europe by the US Secretary of State, General Marshall, 16 western European countries set up a Committee for

European Economic Cooperation which evolved into the Organization for European Economic Cooperation to administer a European Recovery Programme, popularly known as Marshall Aid or the Marshall Plan.

Externality – A positive or negative spill-over effect from consumption or production of one economic agent to another one, based on the non-existence of markets, as in the case of clean air, for which it is impossible to define and enforce property rights.

Foreign direct investment – Investment abroad, usually by transnational corporations, involving an element of control by the investor over the corporation in which the investment is made.

G–7 – Group of Seven; the seven major industrial countries (Canada, France, Italy, Germany, Japan, the United Kingdom and the United States) whose heads of government or economic ministers meet annually at economic summits to coordinate macroeconomic policies, especially exchange rate policies.

G–24 – Group of 24; formed at the 1972 Lima meeting to represent the interests of the developing countries in negotiations on international monetary affairs. The group's members are: Algeria, Argentina, Brazil, Colombia, Côte d'Ivoire, Egypt, Ethiopia, Gabon, Ghana, Guatemala, India, Iran, Lebanon, Mexico, Nigeria, Pakistan, Peru, Philippines, Sri Lanka, Syria, Trinidad and Tobago, Venezuela, the former Yugoslavia and Zaire. China attends as an invitee.

General Agreement on Tariffs and Trade (GATT) – An agreement signed at the 1947 Geneva Conference on multilateral trade. It set out rules of conduct, provided a forum for multilateral negotiations regarding the solution of trade problems and aimed to eliminate tariffs and other barriers to trade.

Generalized System of Preferences (GSP) – Introduced in 1971, the system implies that some exports from developing countries are given preferential access to the markets of industrial countries.

Global Environment Facility (GEF) – An entity that provides grants and concessional funds to developing countries for projects and activities that aim to protect the environment. The GEF Secretariat is functionally independent but administratively supported by the World Bank. The UNDP is responsible for technical assistance activities and UNEP provides the secretariat for the Scientific and Technical Advisory Panel, made up of 15 international environmental experts, which advises on environmental issues and solutions to them.

Gold standard – A system of monetary organization under which the value of a country's money is legally defined as a fixed quantity of gold.

Good governance – Governance which (a) separates clearly between what is public and what is private, (b) implies accountability, (c) is based on the rule of law and (d) implies transparent information and decision making.

Grameen Bank – Established in Bangladesh by Muhammad Yunus, a former university economics professor, as a non-profit development action and research project and formally incorporated under government charter in 1983, the Grameen Bank provides credit without collateral for the poor rural landless laborers, especially women.

Gross domestic product (GDP) – GDP is the value of all final goods and services produced in a country within a given period.

Gross national product (GNP) – GNP is the value of all final goods and services produced by domestically owned factors of production, whether inside or outside the national borders, within a given period.

Human development index (HDI) – A composite measure of human development containing indicators representing three equally weighted dimensions of human development: life expectancy at birth, adult literacy and mean years of schooling, and income per capita in purchasing power parity dollars.

Immiserization – A steady decline in economic welfare. The term was first used by Karl Marx, who predicted an increasing misery of the proletariat, leading to class consciousness and an overthrow of capitalism in a socialist revolution.

Inter-American Development Bank – An international development finance institution, created in 1959 to help accelerate the economic and social development of its member countries in Latin America and the Caribbean. The Bank is owned by its 46 member countries, including 28 regional members from the western Hemisphere, and 18 non-regional members from Europe, Asia and the Middle East. The Bank's headquarters are in Washington, DC.

International Bank for Reconstruction and Development (IBRD) – Commonly referred to as the World Bank, founded in 1944 at Bretton Woods. The lending multilateral development institution, its official aim is to promote long-term economic growth that reduces poverty in developing countries (see also: World Bank Group).

International Development Association (IDA) – An affiliate of the World Bank Group, established in 1960 to promote economic development in the world's poorest countries.

International Finance Corporation (IFC) – The World Bank Group's investment bank for developing countries, established in 1956. It lends directly to private companies and makes equity investments in them, without guarantees from governments.

International Labour Organisation (ILO) – Established in 1919 by the Treaty of Versailles, the ILO became a specialized agency of the United Nations in 1946. The ILO promotes international cooperation regarding policies designed to achieve full employment, improve working conditions, extend social security and raise general living standards.

International Monetary Fund (IMF) – Established in December 1945 following ratification of the Articles of Agreement of the Fund, formulated at the Bretton Woods conference in 1944. The Fund became a specialized agency of the United Nations in 1947 and acts as a monitor of the world's currencies by helping to maintain an orderly system of payments between all countries. To this end, it lends money to its members facing serious balance-of-payments deficits, subject to a variety of conditions.

International Trade Organization (ITO) – In 1947, the United Nations Economic and Social Council (ECOSOC) convened an International Conference on Trade and Development in Havana, Cuba, which drew up the Havana Charter, proposing the establishment of an International Trade Organization under the aegis of the United Nations.

Although 50 countries signed the Havana Charter, it failed to receive the necessary number of ratifications and the idea of a permanent UN trade body was never realized. (See also under GATT, UNCTAD and WTO.)

Keynes Plan – Proposals of the UK treasury to establish an International Clearing Union which received consideration at the Bretton Woods conference in 1944. As John Maynard Keynes (1883–1946) was primarily responsible for their formulation, these proposals were collectively referred to as the Keynes Plan.

Keynesian Revolution – A term used to describe the fundamental change in macroeconomic theory based on John Maynard Keynes' *General Theory of Employment, Interest, and Money* (1936), especially with regard to aggregate demand and its income-generating effect and the possibility of equilibrium with unemployment, both of which discredited the classical and neoclassical dogma of *laissez-faire*.

Marshall Aid – Named after US Secretary of State, General Marshall, the aid given by the United States and Canada to western European countries to restore their economy after World War II, also known as Marshall Plan or European Recovery Programme.

Mixed economy – A system which combines competitive private enterprise with some degree of government activity. While the allocation of resources is dominated by individual actions through the price mechanism, the government plays some role in determining the level of aggregate demand by means of fiscal and monetary policy.

Multilateral Investment Guarantee Agency (MIGA) – A member of the World Bank Group, the MIGA helps to smooth the flow of foreign investment by insuring investors against non-commercial risks and providing investment advice and promotion services.

Neoclassical economics – A body of economic theory which uses the general techniques of the original nineteenth-century marginalist economists. Today, it is often combined with the liberal doctrine, which advocates the greatest possible use of markets and the forces of competition. Thus, economic policy based on neoclassical economics is often called either the neoclassical or the neoliberal paradigm.

Neoclassical synthesis – The synthesis of neoclassical and Keynesian economics, which was developed almost immediately after the publication of Keynes' General Theory in an effort to rescue classical and neoclassical theory while allowing it to absorb some of Keynes' insights.

Net flow of capital – The difference between total flow of capital into and out of a country or institution: the net flow of capital is the gross flow of capital out minus the gross flow of capital in. For example, if the total amount of capital which flows into a country exceeds the total amount of capital which flows out of a country, the country is said to be a net creditor country. Thus the net flow of capital is positive.

Official development assistance (ODA) – Concessional financial aid to developing countries and multilateral institutions provided by official agencies, including state and local governments. It contains at least a grant element of 25 per cent.

Organization for Economic Cooperation and Development (OECD) – Originally set up as the Organization for European Economic Cooperation (OEEC) to coordinate Marshall Plan aid in 1948, the OECD took on its present form in 1961 in order to encourage economic growth and maintain financial stability among its 24 member countries: Australia, Austria, Belgium, Canada, Denmark, Finland, France, Germany, Greece, Iceland, Ireland, Italy, Japan, Luxembourg, the Netherlands, New Zealand, Norway, Portugal, Spain, Sweden, Switzerland, Turkey, the United Kingdom and the United States. Mexico joined in 1994.

Organization for European Economic Cooperation (OEEC) – Following the suggestion by the US Secretary of State, General Marshall, for a program of US assistance to the economic recovery of Europe, 16 European countries set up the Committee of European Economic Cooperation in 1947 to administer and coordinate the European Recovery Programme as the European counterpart to the American Economic Cooperation Administration. The need for a permanent coordinating agency led to the creation of the Organization for European Economic Cooperation (OEEC) in 1948.

Oxfam – A global network of organizations, originating in Oxford, England, that funds self-help projects in developing countries.

Participatory development – Development which includes a mechanism for enabling affected people to share in the creation of a project or program, beginning with identification all the way through to implementation and evaluation. On the national scale it implies a political system of human rights and freedoms, effective governance and increasing democratization.

Policy Framework Paper – The Policy Framework Paper is prepared by borrower countries eligible for funding from the IMF's Enhanced Structural Adjustment Facility (ESAF). It is only adopted after both the IMF and the Bank find the document acceptable. The policies spelled out in this document are the basis on which the IMF provides funds from the ESAF to the country. It may also provide the basis for loans from the World Bank's concessional window, the International Development Association (IDA).

Purchasing power parity (PPP) – A concept which implies in its absolute version that commodities have the same price worldwide when measured in the same currency. The lack of empirical support for the absolute version led to the development of a relative version. The relative version of PPP implies that if prices are rising faster in the domestic economy than in another foreign economy, the domestic currency will go down in value compared to the currency of the foreign economy.

Securities and Exchange Commission (SEC) – An independent agency of the US government established in 1934 to act as the chief regulator of securities, that is, a wide range of financial assets, such as equities. There are five commissioners and a staff of about 1,500.

Social security – Public programs which pay regular amounts of money to workers and their families to make up for income losses associated with old age, illness, unemployment or death.

Special Drawing Right (SDR) – The IMF's standard unit of account which IMF member countries may use to settle international trade balances and debts if the member country meets a variety of conditions. The value of SDRs was originally expressed in terms of gold, but since 1974 it has been valued in its members' currencies.

Structural Adjustment Facility (SAF) – Introduced in 1986, the IMF's provision of resources on concessional terms (0.5 per cent interest per year and repayments within 5–10 years) to low-income developing countries facing balance of payments problems, conditional on a medium-term structural adjustment program, set out in a policy framework paper (PFP). See also: Enhanced Structural Adjustment Facility (ESAF).

Structural Adjustment Program (SAP) – A long-term assistance of the World Bank and other IFIs which is supposed to restore equilibrium and promote economic growth. The original rationale for SAPs was that sound projects were not possible in an unsound policy environment. Thus, SAPs became a new instrument to influence macroeconomic policies of developing countries, based on neoclassical economics, advocating *laissez-faire* and free trade.

Sustainable development – Development which meets the needs of the present generation without compromising the needs of future generations.

Terms of trade – The quotient between an index of export prices and an index for import prices. When a country's terms of trade decline, as is the case for many developing countries, it is necessary to export more in order to import the same quantity of goods and services.

Tobin tax – A proposal first made in 1972 by US Nobel Laureate James Tobin to tax international currency transactions. Tobin's original proposal (1978) suggested imposing a tax of 0.05 per cent on all short-term foreign bank accounts. In his recent proposal in UNDP's *Human Development Report 1994*, Tobin suggests imposing a tax of 0.5 per cent on foreign exchange transactions.

Transnational corporation (TNC) – A large enterprise having a home base in one country but operating wholly or partially-owned subsidiaries in other countries. Such corporations expand internationally to take advantage of economies of scale and to benefit from near-monopoly status.

United Nations Conference on Trade and Development (UNCTAD) – The conference, first convened in 1964, is now a permanent organ of the General Assembly. All members of the United Nations or of its specialized agencies are members of the conference which has a permanent executive organ and a permanent secretariat. Its role has been to protect and champion the case of developing countries against the trade policies of the developed countries. UNCTAD's major success has been in successfully pressing for the Generalized System of Preferences (GSP).

United Nations Development Programme (UNDP) – Created in 1966, it combined the UN Expanded Programme of Technical Assistance and the UN Special Fund. It is responsible for administering and coordinating development projects and technical assistance provided under the auspices of, or the liaison with, the UN system of development agencies and organizations.

Uruguay Round – The eighth round of GATT negotiations, launched in September 1986 in Punta del Este (Uruguay) and finally concluded on April 15, 1994 at Marrakesh (Morocco). It dealt with unfinished business from earlier GATT rounds and new issues, such as trade in services, the protection of intellectual property rights, trade-related investment measures, and especially, the establishment of a World Trade Organization (WTO).

World Bank – See: International Bank for Reconstruction and Development.

World Bank Group – Consists of the International Bank for Reconstruction and Development (IBRD, commonly referred to as the World Bank), the International Finance Corporation (IFC), the International Development Association (IDA), the International Center for Settlements of Investment Disputes (ICSID) and the Multilateral Investment Guarantee Agency (MIGA), all based in Washington, DC.

World Trade Organization (WTO) – The WTO, successor to the GATT, is a procedural umbrella agreement to provide an institutional and organizational framework for the administration of the multilateral trade agreements concluded at GATT's Uruguay Round.

Bibliography

Adams, Patricia 'The World Bank and the IMF in Sub-Saharan Africa: Undermining Development and Environmental Sustainability', in *Journal of International Affairs*, vol. 46, no. 1 (1992), pp. 97–117.

Aditjondro, George 'A Reflection about Past International Advocacy Work on Indonesian Environmental Issues' (mimeo, 1990).

Alston, Philip 'A Third Generation of Solidarity Rights: Progressive Development or Obfuscation of International Human Rights Law?', in *Netherlands International Law Review*, vol. 29 (1982), pp. 307–22.

Americans Talk Issues Foundation *Survey #22: On Improving Democracy in America* (St. Augustine, FL: Americans Talk Issues Foundation, 1993).

Amsden, Alice 'Why Isn't the Whole World Experimenting with the East Asian Model to Develop? Review of *The East Asian Miracle*', in *World Development*, vol. 22, no. 4, April 1994, pp. 627–34.

Bahuguna, Sunderlal *Echoes from the Hills: Save the Himalayan Eco-System: A Call to Humanity* (New Delhi: New Age Printing Press, 1992).

Bahuguna, Sunderlal *Whither Development? Chipko Message, 1994* (Silgara, India: Chipko Information Center, 1994).

Bello, Walden F. *Dark Victory: The United States, Structural Adjustment and Global Poverty* (London: Pluto Press with the Transnational Institute; Oakland: Food First with the Transnational Institute, 1994).

Berle, Jr, Adolf A. and Gardiner C. Means *The Modern Corporation and Private Property* (New York: MacMillan, 1932).

Bhatagar, Bhuvan and Aubrey C. Williams (eds) 'Participatory Development and the World Bank: Potential Directions for Change', in *World Bank Discussion Papers*, no. 183 (Washington, DC: World Bank, 1992).

Bleicher, Samuel A. 'UN vs. IBRD', in *International Organization*, vol. 24 (1970) pp. 31–47.

Bradlow, Daniel D. 'The International Monetary Fund, The World Bank Group and Debt Management', in *Legal Aspects of Debt Management* (Geneva: United Nations Institute of Training and Research, 1993), module V.

Bradlow, Daniel D. 'International Organizations and Private Complaints: The Case of the World Bank Inspection Panel', in *Virginia Journal of International Law*, vol. 34, no. 3 (Spring 1994) pp. 553–613.

Bibliography

Bradlow, Daniel D. (ed.) *International Borrowing*, 3rd edition (Washington, DC: International Law Institute, 1994).

Bradlow, Daniel D. and Claudio Grossman 'Are We Being Propelled Towards a People-Centered Transnational Legal Order?', in *The American University Journal of International Law and Policy*, vol. 9, no. 1 (1993), pp. 1–25.

Braudel, Fernand *Civilization and Capitalism, 15th–18th Century: The Wheels of Commerce*, vol. 2 (New York: Harper & Row, 1982).

Broad, Robin *Unequal Alliance, 1979–1986: The World Bank, the International Monetary Fund, and the Philippines* (Manila: Ateneo de Manila Press, 1988).

Broches, Aron 'Statement of IBRD General Counsel to the Fourth Committee of the UN General Assembly on 28 November 1966', in *International Legal Materials*, vol. 61 (1967) pp. 150–87.

Brown, Bartram S. *The United States and the Politicization of the World Bank: Issues of International Law and Policy* (Geneva: Graduate Institute of International Studies, 1992).

Cairncross, Frances *Costing the Earth* (Cambridge: Harvard Business School Press, 1992).

Calvert Group and Hazel Henderson *The Calvert–Henderson Quality-of-Life Indicators for the United States* (Bethesda, MD: Calvert Group, Inc., forthcoming, Fall 1995).

Cantillon, Richard *Essai Sur la Nature du Commerce en General*, translation by Henry Higgs, July 1931 (London: MacMillan, 1931).

Carson, Rachel *Silent Spring* (Boston: Houghton Mifflin, 1962).

Chandler, Alfred and Takashi Hikino *Scale and Scope: The Dynamics of Industrial Capitalism* (Cambridge, MA: The Belknap Press of Harvard University Press, 1990).

Coase, Ronald H. 'The Nature of the Firm', in Stigler and Boulding (eds), *Readings in Price Theory* (Nashville, TN: American Economic Association, 1952).

Commission of the European Communities, IMF, OECD, United Nations and World Bank *System of National Accounts 1993* (Brussels et al.: Commission of the European Communities et al., 1994).

Cornia, Giovanni A., Richard Jolly and Frances Stewart (eds) *Adjustment With a Human Face – Protecting the Vulnerable and Promoting Growth*, vol. 1, A UNICEF Study (Oxford: Clarendon Press, 1987).

Costanza, Robert (ed.) *Ecological Economics: The Science and Management of Sustainability* (New York: Columbia University Press, 1991).

Culpeper, Roy *Canada and the Global Governors* (Ottawa: The North–South Institute, 1994).

Culpeper, Roy 'Regional Development Banks: Exploiting their Specificity', in *Third World Quarterly*, 1994, vol. 15, no. 3, pp. 459–82.

Culpeper, Roy and Andrew Clark *High Stakes, Low Incomes* (Ottawa: The North–South Institute, 1994).

Daly, Herman E. and John B. Cobb, Jr *For the Common Good: Redirecting the Economy Towards Community, the Environment and a Sustainable Future* (Boston: Beacon Press, 1989).

Deloitte Touche Tohmatsu International and the International Institute of Sustainable Development *Coming Clean: Corporate Environmental Reporting* (London: Touche Ross and Co., 1993).

Demuth, Richard H. 'Relations With Other Multilateral Agencies', in John P. Lewis and Ishan Kapur (eds), *The World Bank Group, Multilateral Aid, and the 1970s* (Lexington, MA: Lexington Books, 1973).

Dizard, Wilson P. and S. Blake Swensrud *Gorbachev's Information Revolution: Controlling Glasnost in a New Electronic Era* (Boulder, CO: Westview Press, 1987).

Drèze, Jean and Amartya Sen *Hunger and Public Action* (Oxford: Clarendon Press; New York: Oxford University Press, 1989).

Edwards, Richard W. *International Monetary Collaboration* (Dobbs Ferry, NY: Transnational Publishers, 1985).

Estes, Richard J. *Trends in World Social Development: The Social Progress of Nations, 1970–1987* (New York: Praeger, 1988).

Feinberg, Richard E. 'The Changing Relationship between the World Bank and the International Monetary Fund', in *International Organization*, vol. 42 (Summer 1988), pp. 545–60.

Frank, Thomas M. 'The Emerging Right to Democratic Governance', in *American Journal of International Law*, vol. 86 (January 1992), pp. 46–91.

Frederick, Howard 'Computer Networks and the Emergence of Global Civil Society', in Linda M. Harasim (ed.) *Global Networks: Computers and International Communication* (Cambridge, MA: Massachusetts Institute of Technology Press, 1993).

Galbraith, John Kenneth *The New Industrial State* (Boston: Houghton Mifflin Company, 1967).

Gerster, Richard 'Accountability of Executive Directors in the Bretton Woods Institutions', in *Journal of World Trade*, vol. 27, no. 6 (1993), pp. 87–116.

Gerster, Richard 'A New Framework for Accountability for the International Monetary Fund', in John Cavanagh, Daphne Wysham and Marcos Arruda (eds), *Beyond Bretton Woods: Alternatives to the Global Economic Order* (London: Pluto Press with the Institute for Policy Studies and the Transnational Institute, 1994) pp. 94–106.

Gillies, David 'Human Rights, Democracy and Good Governance: Stretching the World Bank's Policy Frontiers', in Jo Marie Griesgraber and Bernhard G. Gunter (eds), *Rethinking Bretton Woods*, vol. 3, *The World Bank: Lending on a Global Scale* (London: Pluto Press with the Center of Concern, forthcoming), chapter 5.

Gold, Joseph (ed.) *Legal and Institutional Aspects of the International Monetary System: Selected Essays*, vol. 2 (Washington, DC: International Monetary Fund, 1984).

Griffith-Jones, Stephany and Vassilis Papageorgiou 'Globalization of Financial Markets and Impact on Flows to LDCs: New Challenges for Regulation', in Jo Marie Griesgraber and Bernhard G. Gunter (eds),

Rethinking Bretton Woods, vol. 4, *The World's Monetary System: Towards Stability and Sustainability in the Twenty-first Century* (London: Pluto Press with the Center of Concern, forthcoming), chapter 3.

Grossman, Claudio 'Disappearances in Honduras: The Need for Direct Victim Representation in Human Rights Litigation', in *Hastings International and Comparative Law Review*, vol. 15 (1992) pp. 363–89.

Hampden-Turner, Charles and Fons Trompenaars, *The Seven Cultures of Capitalism* (New York: Doubleday, 1993).

Hannum, Hurst (ed.) *Guide to International Human Rights Practice*, 2nd edition (Philadelphia: University of Pennsylvania Press, 1992).

Harris, Seymour (ed.) *The New Economics: Keynes' Influence on Theory and Public Policy* (New York: Alfred A. Knopf, 1948).

Held, David 'Democracy: From City-states to a Cosmopolitan Order?', in *Political Studies*, vol. XL, Special Issue: Prospects for Democracy, 1992, pp. 10–39.

Helleiner, Gerald K. 'Democracy and Global Governance: Revisiting – and Revising – the Committee of 20', North–South Institute, Speech series (Ottawa: The North–South Institute, 1994).

Henderson, Hazel *Creating Alternative Futures: The End of Economics* (New York: Berkeley Publication Corporation, 1978).

Henderson, Hazel *Politics of the Solar Age: Alternatives to Economics* (Garden City, NY: Anchor Press/Doubleday, 1981).

Henderson, Hazel *Paradigms in Progress* (Indianapolis, IN: Knowledge Systems, 1991).

Henderson, Hazel 'Social Innovation and Citizen Movements', in *Futures*, vol. 25, no. 3 (April 1993) pp. 322–38.

Henkin, Louis *How Nations Behave: Law and Foreign Policy* (New York: Praeger, 1968).

Hettne, Bjorn *Development Theory and the Three Worlds* (London: Longman, 1990).

Hino, Hiroyaki 'IMF–World Bank Collaboration', in *Finance and Development*, vol. 23 (1986), pp. 10–14.

Hutchins, Thomas 'Using the International Court of Justice to Check Human Rights Abuses in World Bank Projects', in *Columbia Human Rights Law Review*, vol. 23 (1991), pp. 487–524.

Hutchinson, Robert A. 'Sunderlal Bahuguna and the Chipko Movement', in *Smithsonian*, vol. 18, no. 11 (February 1988), pp. 184–90.

Inglehart, Ronald *Culture Shift in Advanced Industrial Society* (Princeton, NJ: Princeton University Press, 1990).

International Court of Justice 'Reparation for Injuries Suffered in the Service of the United Nations, Advisory Opinion', in *International Court of Justice Reports, 1949*, p. 174.

International Monetary Fund *World Economic Outlook* and *Addendum* (Washington, DC: International Monetary Fund, 1993).

James, Alan M. 'Unit Veto Dominance in United Nations Peace-Keeping', in Lawrence Finkelstein (ed.), *Politics in The United Nations System* (Durham, NC: Duke University Press, 1988).

Kay, Alan F. and Hazel Henderson 'Policy Document: United Nations Security Insurance Agency (UNSIA)', Participant Paper 2A for Round-table on Global Change, July 22–24, 1994 (St. Augustine, FL: Center for Sustainable Development and Alternative World Futures, 1994).

Kearns, James M. and Turid Sato 'New Practices for Development Professionals', in *Development* (October–December 1989) pp. 109–16.

Kennedy, Paul *The Rise and Fall of the Great Powers: Economic Change and Military Conflict from 1500 to 2000* (New York: Random House, 1987).

Keynes, John Maynard *Collected Writings, Vol. IX: Essays in Persuasion* (London: MacMillan, 1972).

Killick, Anthony and Graham R. Bird (eds) *The IMF and Stabilization: Developing Country Experiences* (New York: St. Martin's Press, 1984).

Knowles, Lilian C.A. *Economic Development in the Nineteenth Century: France, Germany, Russia and the United States* (London: Routledge & Sons, 1932).

Kuhn, Thomas *The Structure of Scientific Revolutions* (Chicago: University of Chicago Press, 1962 and 1970).

Kurtzman, Joel *The Death of Money: How the Electronic Economy has Destabilized the World's Markets and Created Financial Chaos* (New York: Simon and Schuster, 1993).

Lewis, Peter H. 'On the Internet, Dissidents' Shots Heard 'Round the World', in *New York Times*, June 5, 1994, Section E, p. 18.

Lodge, George C. *The New American Ideology* (New York: Alfred A. Knopf, 1975).

Marshall, Alfred *Principles of Economics* (London: Macmillan, 1898).

Max-Neef, Manfred 'Development and Human Needs', in Max-Neef, M. and P. Ekins (eds), *Real Life Economics: Understanding Wealth Creation* (London: Routledge, 1992).

McGrath, Paul 'Delivering Live Aid', in *MacLean's*, vol. 98 (1985), p. 17.

Mead, Walter Russell 'American Economic Policy in the Antemillennial Era', in *World Policy Journal*, vol. 6, no. 3, 1989, pp. 385–468.

Mies, Maria and Vandana Shiva *Ecofeminism* (London: Zed Books, 1993).

Mitchell, Ralph A. and Neil Shafer *Standard Catalog of Depression Scrip of the United States in the 1930s: Including Canada and Mexico* (Iola, WI: Krause Publications, 1985).

Mosley, Paul, Jane Harrigan and John Toye *Aid and Power: The World Bank and Policy-Based Lending*, vol. 1 (London: Routledge, 1991).

Naim, Moises 'The World Bank: Its Role, Governance and Organizational Culture', in *Bretton Woods: Looking to the Future* (Washington, DC: Bretton Woods Commission, July 1994) pp. C–273–87.

Nelson, Brian 'Chipko Revisited', in *Whole Earth Review*, no. 79 (June 22, 1993), pp. 116–21.

Nelson, Joan M. (ed.) *Economic Crisis and Policy Choice: The Politics of Economic Adjustment in Developing Nations* (Princeton, NJ: Princeton University Press, 1990).

Noble, David F. *Forces of Production: A Social History of Industrial Automation* (New York: Alfred A. Knopf, 1984).

Bibliography

North South Roundtable (1993) *The United Nations and the Bretton Woods Institutions: New Challenges for the Twenty-first Century* (Rome: Society for International Development, 1993).

North South Roundtable, Society for International Development *The United Nations and the Bretton Woods Institutions: New Challenges for the 21st Century* (New York: North South Roundtable, Society for International Development, 1993).

O'Connor, John C. 'Towards Environmentally Sustainable Development: Measuring Progress', from the International Union for Conservation of Nature and Natural Resources – World Conservation Union, 19th Session, General Assembly (Buenos Aires, Argentina, January 1994).

Olyers, N. 'Gross Reality of Global Statistics', in *The Weekly Mail and Guardian*, May 13–19, 1994, p. 22.

Organizing for Development, An International Institute (ODII) *The Magic of Interaction* (Washington, DC: ODII, 1994).

Overholt, William H. *The Rise of China* (New York: Norton, 1993).

Owen, Dave (ed.) *Green Reporting* (London, New York: Chapman and Hall, University and Professional Division, 1992).

Özgür, Öztemir A. *Apartheid: The United Nations and Peaceful Change in South Africa* (Dobbs Ferry, NY: Transnational Publishers, 1982).

Paul, Samuel and Arturo Israel (eds) *Non-governmental Organizations and the World Bank* (Washington, DC: World Bank, 1991).

Polanyi, Karl *The Great Transformation* (New York and Toronto: Rinehart & Company, Inc., 1944).

Repetto, Robert *Wasting Assets and Natural Resources in the National Income Accounts* (Washington, DC: World Resources Institute, 1989).

Rodriguez, Nancy 'Redefining Wealth and Progress', in *The Caracas Report on Alternative Development Indicators* (Indianapolis, IN: Knowledge Systems, 1990).

Sato, Turid 'Accountability and the Debt Crisis', in *Futures*, vol. 21, no. 6 (December 1989) pp. 593–607.

Schmidheiny, Stephan *Changing Course: A Global Business Perspective on Development and the Environment* (Cambridge, MA: Massachusetts Institute of Technology Press, 1992).

Sheth, D.L. 'Alternative Development as Political Practice', in *Alternatives*, vol. XII, no. 2, 1987, pp. 155–71.

Shihata, Ibrahim F.I. *The World Bank in a Changing World: Selected Essays* (Boston: Dordrecht; Norwell, MA: M. Nijhoff Publishers, 1991).

Shihata, Ibrahim F.I. 'Human Rights, Development and International Financial Institutions', in *The American University Journal of International Law and Policy*, vol. 8, no. 1 (1992), pp. 27–37.

Shihata, Ibrahim F.I. 'The World Bank and Non-Governmental Organizations', in *Cornell International Law Journal*, vol. 25 (1992), pp. 623–41.

Shiva, Vandana 'From Adjustment to Sustainable Development, the Obstacle of Free Trade', in Ralph Nader *et al.*, *The Case Against Free*

Trade: GATT, NAFTA and the Globalization of Corporate Power (San Francisco: Earth Island Press, 1993).

Shiva, Vandana *Close to Home: Women Reconnect Ecology, Health and Development* (Philadelphia: New Society Publishers, 1994).

Shiva, Vandana 'Beware the Backlash', in *The Guardian*, March 11, 1994, p. 16.

Singer, Hans W. 'Rethinking Bretton Woods: From an Historical Perspective', in Jo Marie Griesgraber and Bernhard G. Gunter (eds), *Rethinking Bretton Woods*, vol. 1, *Promoting Development: Effective Global Institutions for the Twenty-first Century*, (London: Pluto Press with the Center of Concern, 1995), chapter 1.

Singh, Kavaljit and Dalip Swamy *Against Consensus: Three Years of Public Resistance to Structural Adjustment Program* (Delhi: Public Interest Research Group, 1994).

Sitarz, Daniel (ed.) *Agenda 21: The Earth Summit Strategy to Save Our Planet* (Boulder, CO: EarthPress, 1993).

Sivard, Ruth Leger *World Military and Social Expenditures*, 14th edition (Washington, DC: World Priorities, Inc., 1991).

Smith, Kenneth S. 'World Bank, IMF – Do They Help or Hurt Third World?', in *US News and World Report*, April 29, 1985, pp. 43–6.

Smith, William E. 'Planning for the Electricity Sector in Colombia', in Marvin R. Weisbord (ed.), *Discovering Common Ground* (San Francisco: Berret Kohler, 1992).

Smith, William E. *The A–I–C Self-Organizing Process – A Power Purpose Fractal* (Washington, DC: ODII, 1994).

Smith, William E. and Lethem B. Thoolen 'The Design of Organization for Rural Development Projects – A Project Report', *World Bank Staff Working Paper no. 375* (Washington, DC: World Bank, 1980).

Snow, Marcellus S. *The International Telecommunications Satellite Organization, INTELSAT: Economic and Institutional Challenges Facing an International Organization* (Huntsville, AL: International Book Import Service, Inc., 1987).

South Commission *The Challenge to the South: Report of the South Commission* (London and New York: Oxford University Press, 1990).

Studenski, Paul *The Income of Nations: Theory, Measurement and Analysis: Past and Present; A Study in Applied Economics and Statistics* (New York: New York University Press, 1958).

Tomasevski, Katarina 'Human Rights Impact Assessment: Proposals for the Next 50 Years of Bretton Woods', in Jo Marie Griesgraber and Bernhard G. Gunter (eds), *Rethinking Bretton Woods*, vol. 1, *Promoting Development: Effective Global Institutions for the Twenty-first Century* (London: Pluto Press with the Center of Concern, 1995), chapter 4.

Ulrich von Weisäcker, Ernst *Ecological Tax Reform* (London: Zed Books, 1992).

United Nations *Agenda 21, UNCED Concluding Document: Press Summary* (New York: United Nations Department of Public Information, 1992).

Bibliography

United Nations Development Programme *Human Development Report 1992* (New York: Oxford University Press, 1992).

United Nations Development Programme *Human Development Report 1994* (New York: Oxford University Press, 1995).

United Nations Statistical Division *Handbook of National Accounting: Integrated Environmental and Economic Accounting* (New York: United Nations, 1993).

United States Department of Commerce 'Integrated Economic and Environmental Satellite Accounts', in *Survey of Current Business*, vol. 74, no. 4 (April 1994), pp. 33–49.

Urdaneta-Ferrán, Lourdes 'Rethinking Statistical Requirements: Gender Statistics and Accounts', in Jo Marie Griesgraber and Bernhard G. Gunter (eds), *Rethinking Bretton Woods*, vol. 1, *Promoting Development: Effective Global Institutions for the Twenty-first Century* (London: Pluto Press with the Center of Concern, 1995), chapter 5.

Wachtel, Howard *The Money Mandarins: The Making of a Supranational Economic Order* (London: Pluto Press, 1990; Armonk, NY: M.E. Sharpe, 1990).

Walker, Martin *The Waking Giant: Gorbachev's Russia* (New York: Pantheon Books, 1986).

Wallich, Paul 'Lies, Damned Lies and Models', in *Scientific American*, January 1994, p. 151.

Waring, Marilyn *If Women Counted* (San Francisco: Harpers, 1988).

Weiss, Edith B. *Fairness to Future Generations: International Law, Common Patrimony and Intergenerational Equity* (Tokyo: United Nations University; Dobbs Ferry, NY: Transnational Publishers, 1989).

Westley, Frances 'Bob Geldof and Live Aid: The Effective Side of Global Social Innovation', in *Human Relations*, vol. 44 (1991), pp. 1011–36.

World Bank *World Bank Operational Directive 2.20* (Washington, DC: World Bank, October 1989).

World Bank, *Governance and Development* (Washington, DC: World Bank, 1992).

World Bank *The East Asian Miracle* (New York: Oxford University Press, 1993).

World Bank *Adjustment in Africa* (New York: Oxford University Press, 1994).

World Bank *Sourcebook on Participation* (Washington, DC: World Bank; Draft, December 1994) Section on Colombia Energy Sector Reforms.

World Bank *World Bank Annual Report 1994* (Washington, DC: World Bank, 1994).

World Commission on Environment and Development *Our Common Future* (Oxford and New York: Oxford University Press, 1987).

Notes on Contributors

Daniel D. Bradlow is an Associate Professor of Law at the American University in Washington, DC, where he specializes in international economic law. His current work focuses on the international financial institutions and the international legal aspects of economic development. He is a Senior Special Fellow on the legal aspects of debt management at the United Nations Institute of Training and Research (UNITAR). Prior to joining the American University, Professor Bradlow worked as a Research Associate at the International Law Institute, as a consultant to the United Nations Center on Transnational Corporations and as a lawyer in private practice.

Roy Culpeper received his Ph.D. in Economics from the University of Toronto in 1975. Between 1975 and 1978 he worked for the Manitoba Government (with the Cabinet Planning Secretariat) and for the federal Department of Finance (on Canadian economic development policy) between 1978 and 1981. After being seconded to External Affairs for two years where he worked on the department's World Bank desk, he was posted to the World Bank in Washington where he was advisor to the Canadian Executive Director. Since 1986 he has been at the North–South Institute, directing the Institute's research on international debt and finance. He was named the Institute's vice-president in 1991.

Claudio Grossman is Dean of Graduate Studies at the Washington College of Law and First Vice-President of the Inter-American Commission on Human Rights. He has written and practiced extensively in the area of international human rights law. As a member of the Inter-American Commission, he has decided on petitions on freedom of expression and information. He teaches International Law and International Protection of Human Rights and has recently published 'Are We Being Propelled Towards a People-Centered Transnational Legal Order?' in *The American University Journal of International Law and Policy*.

Hazel Henderson, an independent sustainable development policy analyst since 1970, served on the original Advisory Council of the US Office of Technology Assessment from 1974 to 1980. She has had over 250 articles published in many professional international journals and her editorials are syndicated in 27 languages by Inter Press Service (IPS, Rome) to some 400 newspapers. Henderson has been a Regent's Lecturer at the University of California (Santa Barbara) and held the Horace Albright Chair at the University of California (Berkeley) in 1982. Currently, she serves on the Business Council for the UN World Summit on Social Development (BUSCO, Paris), the Task Force on Efficient Capital Markets of the Business Council for Sustainable Development (Geneva), and is a Commissioner of the Global Commission to Fund the UN (Washington, DC).

Lisa Jordan works with BothENDs, an environment and development service organization in the Netherlands, where she coordinates the Multilateral Financial Institutions Program to promote the democratization of multilateral institutions. Prior to joining BothENDs, Ms Jordan was Director of GLOBE-US (Global Legislators Organization for a Balanced Environment) and served as Legislative Assistant to US Representative James H. Scheuer, then chairman of the Subcommittee on the Environment of the House Committee on Science, Space and Technology. With the subcommittee, Jordan worked on international environmental issues and prepared the first public hearing on the Sardar Sarovar Dam Project in India. Ms Jordan holds an M.A. in development studies from the Institute of Social Studies in The Hague, Netherlands. She has written numerous articles on democracy, international power relations, debt and trade.

Sixto K. Roxas After a long career in government and in private business, in the Philippines and abroad, Sixto Roxas retired from merchant banking in 1982 to create the Foundation for Community Organization and Management Technology (FCOMT). Through FCOMT and his active service with numerous other nongovernmental organizations (including the Green Forum Philippines, the Sustainable Development Network and the Foundation for Philippine Environment) Roxas is engaged in translating sustainable development into operational protocols at the community level. He also serves on a number of international task forces and steering committees, such as the Vietnam–ASEAN Task Force, and the Prince of Wales Business Leader Forum.

Roxas received his academic degree in development economics

at Fordham University in New York in 1954. He served as chief economist at the Philippine National Bank and executive vice-president of the first Philippine oil company, Filoil Refinery Corp., before becoming cabinet secretary for economic planning under President Macapagal. He was also chairman of the National Economic Council, governor of the Land Authority in charge of agrarian reform agencies, and founder of the Economic Development Foundation. After leaving government, he established an Asian merchant banking group (Bancom, 1965), was president and then co-chairman of the Asian Institute of Management (1975–86), and founded the Philippines' Business for Social Progress. He served as vice-chairman of the American Express International Banking Corporation in New York (1978–80) and chairman of the merchant banking subsidiary of American Express in London (1978).

Turid Sato, a student of Joseph Campbell at Sarah Lawrence College and of Barbara Ward at Columbia School of International and Public Affairs, joined the World Bank as a young professional in 1970. While on a sabbatical at the Massachusetts Institute of Technology's Sloan School, she became fluent in designing and managing stakeholder processes to achieve better results. Unable to convince the Bank to adopt a more democratic approach to project identification and preparation, she left in 1987 to help establish Organizing for Development, an International Institute (ODII), located in Washington, DC. She believes:

After 25 years in development, I have come to conclude that the current model of development is fundamentally flawed. Transfer of resources is not sufficient; while it may be spurred by catalytic forces from the environment, development is a process that comes from within. People and countries have to take responsibility for their own development, for the design and implementation of the visions and priorities that will create the kind of community they would like to leave for future generations. Thus, the role of development assistance must change to encourage more participatory processes in support of the overall goal of enhancing the countries and communities own ability to develop themselves.

William E. Smith is a thinker and practitioner in the field of organization. Dr Smith's innovations were first evident when, as manager for British Airways, he made Rome the best performing of all BOAC's stations in less than six months and without managerial control or expenditure of additional resources. In search for the principles that led to this performance, he pursued a career in consulting, worked for a multinational pharmaceutical company, obtained a Ph.D. at the Wharton Graduate School of Business and then applied the results to the design of development projects at the World Bank.

The principles which can be applied to any form of organization are expressed as an organizing philosophy and model called AIC – Appreciation, Influence, and Control – an approach which focuses on the fundamental power relationships required for the successful accomplishment of any complex purpose. The approach has been applied at every level of the organizational hierarchy, from village development to regional to international development, culminating with a global workshop on the New Development Paradigm discussed in Chapter 5.

Rethinking Bretton Woods

PROJECT SPONSORS

Charles Abugre
Third World Network
GHANA

Adebayo Adedeji
African Centre for Development and Strategic Studies
NIGERIA

Peggy Antrobus
Development Alternatives with Women for a New Era (DAWN)
BARBADOS

Tissa Balasuriya, OMI
Centre for Society and Religion
SRI LANKA

David Barkin *
Lincoln Institute of Land Policy
Cambridge, MA and MEXICO

Leonor Briones
Freedom from Debt Coalition
PHILIPPINES

Edward Broadbent and **David Gillies**
International Centre for Human Rights
and Democratic Development
CANADA

Salvie D. Colina
Asian Center for the Progress of Peoples
HONG KONG

Snuuth Fernando
Devasarana Development Centre
SRI LANKA

Susan Fleck and Bernhard Gunter
Economics Graduate Student Union
The American University
Washington, DC USA

Louis Goodman
Dean, School of International Service
The American University
Washington, DC USA

J. Bryan Hehir *
Harvard University
Cambridge, MA USA

Gabriel Izquierdo, SJ
Centro de Investigación y Educación Popular (CINEP)
COLOMBIA

Fatima Mello
Federation of Organizations for Social and Educational Assistance
(FASE)
BRAZIL

Guy Mhone
Southern Africa Regional Institute for Policy Studies
ZIMBABWE

Luis Peirano and Humberto Campodonico
Centro de Estudios y Promoción del Desarrollo (DESCO)
PERU

Sebasti L. Raj, SJ
Indian Social Institute
INDIA

Jorge Sábato *
Centro de Estudios Avanzados
ARGENTINA

Francisco Sagasti
Grupo de Analisis para el Desarrollo (GRADE)
PERU

Tom Schlesinger
Southern Finance Project
Philomont, VA USA

Kavaljit Singh
Public Interest Research Group
INDIA

Rob van Drimmelen
World Council of Churches
SWITZERLAND

Peter van Tuijl and Augustinus Rumansara
International NGO Forum on Indonesian Development
INDONESIA / THE NETHERLANDS

Layashi Yaker
United Nations Economic Commission for Africa
ETHIOPIA

Noel Keizo Yamada, SJ
Sophia University
JAPAN

* Personal capacity, organization listed for identification only.

PROJECT ADVISORY GROUP

Nii Akwuettah
Africa Development Foundation

Nancy Alexander
Bread for the World Institute

Steven Arnold
Professor, School of International Service
The American University

Ambassador Richard Bernal
Embassy of Jamaica

Daniel Bradlow
Professor, Washington College of Law
The American University

Robert Browne
Economic Consultant

Margaret Crahan
Luce Professor of Religion, Power and Political Process
Occidental College, Los Angeles

Maria Floro
Professor, Department of Economics
The American University

Louis Goodman
Dean, School of International Service
The American University

Jo Marie Griesgraber
Project Director, Center of Concern

Chandra Hardy
International Development Training Institution

James E. Hug, SJ
Director, Center of Concern

Constantine Michalopoulos
The World Bank

Moises Naim
Senior Fellow, Carnegie Endowment for International Peace

Ambassador Margaret Taylor
Embassy of Papua New Guinea

Marijke Torfs
Friends of the Earth

Index

Note: For acronyms see list on
p. xi. Figures and Tables are given
in **bold**. *Italic* page numbers refer to
the Glossary.

developing countries *continued*
influence of 91, 119
development: lack of capital for 77;
measured by GNP xiv, xv–xvi,
52n; multi-dimensional 65, 82;
people's control over 68, 96, 97,
99; purpose of 83, 95; traditional
BWI model xviii, 5–6, 11, 25n,
94–5, 5.2, *see also* development
paradigm (new); sustainable
development
development facility, proposed
99–100
development paradigm (new)
xiv–xv, xvii, 89–90, 103; diversity
of xviii; exemplar (Thai Foundation) 95–6, 97, 100; meta-
theory of 90, 92–5, 5.1, 5.2;
preconditions of 16–19, 91,
100–2; recommendations for
institutions 97–9; role of stakeholders 95, 97
devolution, principle of 67, 71, 72,
99
Dobb, Maurice 24n
Dodge Plan xiii

Earth Summit *see* UNCED
Earth System Science model **Table
6.2**
EBRD 61, 73n
ecology: political problems of
126–7; responsibility for 16; and
sustainability 12–13, 15, *see also*
environment
economic indicators: analysis of
124–5; new 115–19; politics and
119–23; role of xv–xvi, 103–31;
traditional 115
economic theory 3, 106, 113–15;
ideology of 10, 83, *see also* classical economics; Keynesian economics; neoclassical economics
Economist, The 108, 116
EDP (environmentally adjusted net
domestic product) 117–18
employment: and cheap labor 108;

employment *continued*
and economic growth 107–8,
116, 131n; full (as economic
goal) 5; Jobs Summit (Detroit)
109–10, *see also* NAIRU
enterprise economics: and accounting systems 15; globalization of
1, 7–9; infrastructure of 10–11;
predominance of 8–9
enterprise management 15–16
entrepeneur, role of 7, 24n
environment: economic definitions
of 81, 126–7; indicators in SNA
107, 110, 116–19; international
concern about 33, 37–8, 105;
pollution control 117, 127; totality of 29, 77, 81, *see also* ecology
environmental impact assessments
64
environmental treaties, legal principles of xvi
equalization 20
Estes, Richard J. 115
Europe, economic system 2–3
European Union, and *SNA 1993*
118

'Fifty Years is Enough' campaign
60, 76, 87n, 121
Finance and Development (World
Bank) 63
financial institutions: redefinition
of role 18–19, *see also* banking
Ford Foundation 129

G–7 countries 86, 110, *140*; economic failures of 79; and Jobs
Summit 109
Galbraith, John Kenneth 8
GATT 78, 121, *140*
GDP *141*; in accounting systems
105, 115, 118–19; criticism of
121–2; growth policies 107–8;
sustainable development indicators in 125–8, *see also* economic
indicators; GNP
GEF 59n, 64, 129, *140*